AF802635

Choir Director's Organizer

2005–2006

Abingdon Press
Nashville, Tennessee

Contents

CHOIR DIRECTOR'S ORGANIZER
2005–2006

This book is printed on acid-free, recycled paper.

ISBN 0-687-05567-9

05 06 07 08 09 10 11 12 13 14 — 10 9 8 7 6 5 4 3 2 1

Manufactured in the United States of America

Introduction and Instructions

Theme: "Then Sings My Soul."

Many choir directors are excellent organizers. Many others can use some organizational assistance. All can benefit from some or all of the helpful items in this kit. Some directors may wish to purchase a standard three-ring binder to keep all the forms handy and in a preferred order.

Pages specified "reproducible" may be copied for your use and convenience. Make copies of whatever you need, keeping the originals in a safe place for when you need to make more. If these forms need only minor adjustments to meet your needs, consider making a copy of the form and "whiting out" the sections you do not need. Make one more copy and you have a new form that will fit your needs exactly!

Choir Year Theme. This year's theme, "Then Sings My Soul," can be a part of all your newsletters, mailings, posters, and other choir materials for the whole year. This will help make your ministry easily recognizable to the choir participants and church members alike. Reproducible clip art and a choir certificate will help you develop this theme throughout the year.

Here is what you will find in the kit and some ideas and instructions about how to use each item:

Worship Music Planners. There is one for traditional worship services and one for blended or contemporary worship services. Use these to project your thinking several weeks (or even months) in advance as you consider upcoming seasons, topics, or themes in planning and selecting music for worship.

Rehearsal Planning Worksheets. There is one for children's choirs, one for youth choirs, one for adult choirs, and one for instrumental/bell ensembles. Use these to map out your rehearsals so that sufficient rehearsal time is allocated to each upcoming piece of music.

Choir Registration Form. At the beginning of the choir year have the youth and adult members of the music program fill out one form each, and have the parents of the children (and possibly of the youth) fill one out for each of their children. Then throughout the year have new members and parents fill them out when they join.

Alphabetize the forms and keep them in a notebook. You might consider duplicating the forms and keeping this second set organized by musical group.

You might also use this as a template for designing your own computerized database of choir members.

Sample Letters. The sample letters incorporate the choir year theme: "Then Sings My Soul." Includes a variety of kinds of letters and postcards for adults, youth, children, and handbell choirs/instrumental groups.

These are intended to stimulate your imagination and encourage frequent personal communication between director and members of the choir program. Adapt them to your specific needs.

Clip Art. **All art is reproducible.**

A reproducible certificate of appreciation is included that uses the choir year theme. Consider using different colors of paper for different choirs.

These will help "spice up" your newsletters, bulletins, posters, and personal correspondence. Cut and paste to your heart's delight.

Calendars. There is one three-years-at-a-glance calendar on a single page, and thirteen two-page monthly calendars (August 2005 through August 2006) for detailed planning. These can be used for your personal planning. You can also write significant events on blank calendar pages and copy them for your choir members. Scripture passages listed on Sundays are taken from the Revised Common Lectionary for those churches that use it.

Hymn Usage Chart. This is an alphabetized list of hymns and praise choruses common to several denominational and ecumenical hymnals.

There are also several lines at the end of the chart on which to add hymns, songs, choruses, and so on, which do not appear in the hymnal.

These forms will last one year. You may simply check the box when a particular selection is used, or you may use the following key (or one you create) to indicate how it was used.

M   Morning worship (M1 or M2 if you have two services using different music)

E Evening worship
W Weekday or weeknight service
C Choral use
S Solo use (D for duet, T for Trio, and so forth)
I Instrumental use (or H for handbell use, O for orchestral use, and so forth)

You can also use these pages as a planning tool, mapping out congregational music in advance to ensure the balance of old and new hymns you desire.

Music Library Card. This can be stored as separate sheets or duplicated onto 5″ x 7″ card stock. Duplicate this page for each anthem, collection, and major work in your music library.

Assign a library number to each title. Choose the season(s) of the church year that best suits this work. Note the accompaniment (required and optional) in the space labeled “Instrumentation.” The “Category” provides a way to identify if the work is an anthem, call to worship, handbell piece, collection, oratorio, and so on. If possible, store your music by consecutive library number, no matter what the category. This will make for easy locating by the next director, as well as the most efficient use of space.

Once completed, you may want to duplicate the sheet twice, filing the original by library number, and the duplicates alphabetically by title and composer/arranger, respectively. You may also want to use various colors of papers to indicate the seasons of the church year (green for Christmas, for example).

Instrument and Equipment Chart. This will be helpful to keep up with existing as well as newly purchased instruments and equipment, may be helpful in the budget planning process, and may be necessary for insurance purposes.

Music Department Budget Form. Make copies of the worksheet for other music committee members helping plan next year’s budget. This will help you and the committee consider all facets of budgeting for the next year.

Choir Robe and Folder Assignment Charts. There is one for choir robes, one for choir folders, and one for those who prefer to combine the robe and folder information on one chart.

Write robe and folder numbers on the charts and then post them near the area where the robes and folders are stored. You may want to write the numbers in ink, then laminate the sheets before adding members’ names with an erasable marker. This will allow for changes that invariably happen during the year.

Attendance Records. There is a format for adult, handbell/instrumental choirs and one for children’s and youth choirs. A “second” page is included to be used with *all* choirs. Make at least one copy of the “second” page for each choir.

Tape a “second” page onto the right-hand edge of each “first” page so the lines match; the three-hole punching will allow you to fold the two pages together and still fit them into a three-ring binder.

Write the dates in the triangles across the top line. Each box is divided into two triangles, one for the weekly rehearsal, and one for Sunday worship. Write in only the dates that apply to each individual choir (for example, a children’s choir may rehearse every week, but sing for worship only a few times a year). You might also want to keep one attendance record of rehearsals and another of worship services for those groups that sing most frequently.

Fill in the names, addresses, phone numbers, and birth dates (and grade in school of children and youth). Place a check mark in the appropriate triangle when the choir member is present; leave blank if absent. Fill in the totals for each date at the end of rehearsals and services.

Clip Art

Worship Music Planner (Traditional)

Date ______________________ Time ______________

Liturgical Season and Sunday ______________________

Color/Visual Focus ______________________

Scripture(s)/Theme/Sermon Topic ______________________

____

Congregational Service Music

Opening Hymn No. ________ Tune ____________ Title ____________

Middle Hymn No. ________ Tune ____________ Title ____________

Closing Hymn No. ________ Tune ____________ Title ____________

Praise Choruses______________________

Music during Communion______________________

Other ______________________

Service Music

Introit/Call to Worship ______________________

Prayer Call or Response ______________________

Anthem (1) ______________________

Anthem (2) ______________________

Benediction Response ______________________

Solo/Special Music ______________________

Other ______________________

Instrumental Music

Opening Prelude/Voluntary ______________________

Offertory ______________________

Closing Postlude/Voluntary ______________________

Other ______________________

Notes:

Worship Music Planner (Blended/Contemporary)

Date ______________________________ Time ____________________

Scripture(s)/Theme ____

____

Visuals/Colors ____

Praise and Worship Choruses

Title/Hymn	Songbook	Page No.	Tempo	Style	Key

Other Music

Opening Song ____

Prayer Song ____

Solo ____

Choir/Praise Team Anthem ____

Closing Song ____

Other ____

Instrumental Music

Instrumentalists/instruments available _________________________________

Before Worship ____

Offertory ____

After Worship ____

Other ____

Drama Ideas and Notes:

Clip Art

Important Dates 2005–2006

Advent begins	November 27, 2005
Christmas Eve/Day	December 24/25, 2005
Epiphany	January 6, 2006
Ash Wednesday	February 1, 2006
Palm Sunday	April 9, 2006
Good Friday	April 14, 2006
Easter	April 16, 2006
Pentecost	June 4, 2006

AUGUST 2005

SUNDAY	MONDAY	TUESDAY
Notes for August:	1	2
7 O. Gen. 37:1-4, 12-28 P. Ps. 105:1-6, 16-22, 45*b* E. Rom. 10:5-15 G. Matt. 14:22-33 Green	8	9
14 O. Gen 45:1-15 P. Ps. 133 E. Rom 11:1-2*a*, 29-32 G. Matt. 15:(10-20), 21-28 Green	15	16
21 O. Exod. 1:8–2:10 P. Ps. 124 E. Rom. 12:1-8 G. Matt. 16:13-20 Green	22	23
28 O. Exod. 3:1-15 P. Ps. 105:1-6, 23-26, 45*c* E. Rom. 12:9-21 G. Matt. 16:21-28 Green	29	30

AUGUST 2005

WEDNESDAY	THURSDAY	FRIDAY	SATURDAY
3	4	5	6
10	11	12	13
17	18	19	20
24	25	26	27
31	Notes:		

SEPTEMBER 2005

SUNDAY	MONDAY	TUESDAY
Notes for September:		
4 O. Exod. 12:1-14 P. Ps. 149 E. Rom. 13:8-14 G. Matt. 18:15-20 Green	**5** Labor Day	**6**
11 O. Exod. 14:19-31 P. Ps. 114 E. Rom. 14:1-12 G. Matt. 18:21-35 Green	**12**	**13**
18 O. Exod. 16:2-15 P. Ps. 105:1-6, 37-45 E. Phil. 1:21-30 G. Matt. 20:1-16 Green	**19**	**20**
25 O. Exod. 17:1-7 P. Ps. 78:1-4, 12-16 E. Phil. 2:1-13 G. Matt. 21:23-32 Green	**26**	**27**

SEPTEMBER 2005

WEDNESDAY	THURSDAY	FRIDAY	SATURDAY
Notes: ______	1	2	3
7	8	9	10
14	15	16	17
21	22 First Day of Autumn	23	24
28	29	30	

OCTOBER 2005

SUNDAY	MONDAY	TUESDAY
Notes for October:		
2 World Communion Sunday O. Exod. 20:1-4, 7-9, 12-20 P. Ps. 19 E. Phil. 3:4*b*-14 G. Matt. 21:33-46 Green	**3** Rosh Hashanah	**4**
9 O. Exod. 32:1-14 P. Ps.106:1-6, 19-23 E. Phil. 4:1-9 G. Matt. 22:1-14 Green	**10**	**11**
16 O. Exod. 33:12-23 P. Ps. 99 E. 1 Thess. 1:1-10 G. Matt. 22:15-22 Green	**17**	**18**
23 O. Deut. 34:1-12 P. Ps. 90:1-6, 13-17 E. 1 Thess. 2:1-8 G. Matt. 22:34-46 Green	**24**	**25**
30 Reformation Sunday O. Josh. 3:7-17 P. Ps. 107:1-7, 33-37 E. 1 Thess. 2:9-13 G. Matt. 23:1-12 Green	**31**	

OCTOBER 2005

WEDNESDAY	THURSDAY	FRIDAY	SATURDAY
Notes:			1
5	6	7	8
12 Columbus Day	13 Yom Kippur	14	15
19	20	21	22
26	27	28	29

Notes:

NOVEMBER 2005

SUNDAY	MONDAY	TUESDAY
Notes for November:		1 All Saints Day White
6 O. Josh. 24:1-3a, 14-25 P. Ps. 78:1-7 E. 1 Thess. 4:13-18 G. Matt. 25:1-13 Green	7	8
13 O. Judg. 4:1-7 P. Ps. 123 E. 1 Thess. 5:1-11 G. Matt. 25:14-30 Green	14	15
20 Christ the King/Reign of Christ Sunday O. Ezek. 34:11-16, 20-24 P. Ps. 100 E. Eph. 1:15-23 G. Matt. 25:31-46 White	21	22
27 Advent 1 O. Isa. 64:1-9 P. Ps. 80:1-7, 17-19 E. 1 Cor. 1:3-9 G. Mark 13:24-37 Purple	28	29

NOVEMBER 2005

WEDNESDAY	THURSDAY	FRIDAY	SATURDAY
2	3	4	5
9	10	11 Veterans Day	12
16	17	18	19
23	24 Thanksgiving Day	25	26
30	Notes:		

DECEMBER 2005

SUNDAY	MONDAY	TUESDAY
Notes for December:		
4 Advent 2 O. Isa. 40:1-11 P. Ps. 85:1-2, 8-13 E. 2 Pet. 3:8-15*a* G. Matt. 1:1-8 Purple	**5**	**6**
11 Advent 3 O. Isa. 61:1-4, 8-11 P. Ps. 126 E. 1 Thess. 5:16-24 G. John 1:6-8, 19-28 Purple	**12**	**13**
18 Advent 4 O. 2 Sam. 7:1-11, 16 P. Luke 1:47-55 E. Rom. 16:25-27 G. Luke 1:26-38 Purple	**19**	**20**
25 Christmas Day O. Isa. 52:7-10 P. Ps. 98 E. Heb. !:1-4, (5-12) G. John 1:1-14 White	**26** Hanukkah begins	**27**

DECEMBER 2005

WEDNESDAY	THURSDAY	FRIDAY	SATURDAY
Notes:	1	2	3
7	8	9	10
14	15	16	17
21 First Day of Winter	22	23	24 Christmas Eve Purple (A.M.) White (P.M.)
28	29	30	31 New Year's Eve White

JANUARY 2006

SUNDAY	MONDAY	TUESDAY
1 New Year's Day O. Isa. 61:1–62:3 P. Ps. 148 E. Gal. 4:4-7 G. Luke 2:22-40 White	**2**	**3**
8 Baptism of the Lord O. Gen. 1:1-5 P. Ps. 29 E. Acts 19:1-7 G. Mark 1:4-11 White	**9**	**10**
15 O. 1 Sam. 3:1-10, (11-20) P. Ps. 139:1-6, 13-18 E. 1 Cor. 6:12-20 G. John 1:43-51 Green	**16** Martin Luther King Jr. Day	**17**
22 Week of Prayer for Christian Unity O. Jon. 3:1-5, 10 P. Ps. 62:5-12 E. 1 Cor. 7:29-31 G. Mark 1:14-20 Green	**23**	**24**
29 O. Deut. 18:15-20 P. Ps. 111 E. 1 Cor. 8:1-13 G. Mark 1:21-28 Green	**30**	**31**

JANUARY 2006

WEDNESDAY	THURSDAY	FRIDAY	SATURDAY
4	5	6 Epiphany	7
11	12	13	14
18	19	20	21
25	26	27	28

Notes for January: ______________________________

____

____

____

____

____

FEBRUARY 2006

SUNDAY	MONDAY	TUESDAY
Notes for February:		
5 O. Isa. 40:21-31 P. Ps. 147:1-11, 20*c* E. 1 Cor. 9:16-23 G. Mark 1:29-39 Green	**6**	**7**
12 O. 2 Kings 5:1-14 P. Ps. 30 E. 1 Cor. 9:24-27 G. Mark 1:40-45 Green	**13**	**14** Valentine's Day
19 O. Isa. 40:18-25 P. Ps. 41 E. 2 Cor. 1:18-22 G. Mark 2:1-12 Green	**20** President's Day	**21**
26 Transfiguration Sunday O. 2 Kings 2:1-12 P. Ps. 50:1-6 E. 2 Cor. 4:3-6 G. Mark 9:2-9 White	**27**	**28**

FEBRUARY 2006

WEDNESDAY	THURSDAY	FRIDAY	SATURDAY
1 Ash Wednesday Purple	2	3	4
8	9	10	11
15	16	17	18
22	23	24	25

Notes:

MARCH 2006

SUNDAY	MONDAY	TUESDAY
Notes for March:		
5 O. Gen. 9:8-17 P. Ps. 25:1-10 E. 1 Pet. 3:18-22 G. Mark 1:9-15 Purple	**6**	**7**
12 O. Gen. 17:1-7, 15-16 P. Ps. 22:23-31 E. Rom. 4:13-25 G. Mark 8:31-38 Purple	**13**	**14**
19 O. Exod. 20:1-17 P. Ps. 19 E. 1 Cor. 1:18-25 G. John 2:13-22 Purple	**20**	**21** First Day of Spring
26 O. Num. 21:4-9 P. Ps. 107:1-3, 17-22 E. Eph. 2:1-10 G. John 3:14-21 Purple	**27**	**28**

MARCH 2006

WEDNESDAY	THURSDAY	FRIDAY	SATURDAY
1	2	3	4
8	9	10	11
15	16	17 St. Patrick's Day	18
22	23	24	25
29	30	31	

APRIL 2006

SUNDAY	MONDAY	TUESDAY
Notes for April:		
2 O. Jer. 31:31-34 P. Ps. 51:1-12 E. Heb. 5:5-10 G. John 12:20-33 Purple	**3**	**4**
9 Passion/Palm Sunday O. Mark 11:1-11 (Palms) Isa. 50:4-9*a* (Passion) P. Ps. 118:1-2, 19-29 (Palms) Ps. 31:9-16 (Passion) E. Phil. 2:5-11 G. Mark 14:1–15:47 Purple	**10**	**11**
16 Easter Sunday O. Acts 10:34-43 P. Ps. 118:1-2, 14-24 E. 1 Cor. 15:1-11 G. John 20:1-18 White	**17**	**18**
23 O. Acts 4:32-35 P. Ps. 133 E. 1 John 1:1–2:2 G. John 20:19-31 White	**24**	**25**
30 O. Acts 3:12-19 P. Ps. 4 E. 1 John 3:1-7 G. Luke 24:36*b*-48 White	Notes:	

APRIL 2006

WEDNESDAY	THURSDAY	FRIDAY	SATURDAY
Notes:			1
5	6	7	8
12	13 Holy Thursday Purple	14 Good Friday	15
19	20	21	22
26	27	28	29

Notes:

MAY 2006

SUNDAY	MONDAY	TUESDAY
Notes for May:	**1**	**2**
7 O. Acts 4:5-12 P. Ps. 23 E. 1 John 3:16-24 G. John 10:11-18 White	**8**	**9**
14 Mother's Day O. Acts 8:26-40 P. Ps. 22:25-31 E. 1 John 4:7-21 G. John 15:1-8 White	**15**	**16**
21 O. Acts 10:44-48 P. Ps. 98 E. 1 John 5:1-6 G. John 15:9-17 White	**22**	**23**
28 Ascension Sunday O. Acts 1:1-11 P. Ps. 47 E. Eph. 1:15-23 G. Luke 24:44-53 White	**29** Memorial Day, observed	**30**

MAY 2006

WEDNESDAY	THURSDAY	FRIDAY	SATURDAY
3	4	5	6
10	11	12	13
17	18	19	20
24	25	26	27
31	Notes for May:		

JUNE 2006

SUNDAY	MONDAY	TUESDAY
Notes for June:		
4 Pentecost Sunday O. Acts 2:1-21 P. Ps. 104:24-34, 35*b* E. Rom. 8:22-27 G. John 15:26-27, 16:4*b*-15 Red	**5**	**6**
11 Trinity Sunday O. Isa. 6:1-8 P. Ps. 29 E. Rom. 8:12-17 G. John 3:1-17 White	**12**	**13**
18 Father's Day O. 1 Sam. 15:34–16:13 P. Ps. 20 E. 2 Cor. 5:6-10, (11-13), 14-17 G. Mark 4:26-34 Green	**19**	**20**
25 O. 1 Sam. 17:(1*a*, 4-11, 19-23) P. Ps. 9:9-20 E. 2 Cor. 6:1-13 G. Mark 4:35-41 Green	**26**	**27**

JUNE 2006

WEDNESDAY	THURSDAY	FRIDAY	SATURDAY
Notes: ______	1	2	3
7	8	9	10
14 Flag Day	15	16	17
21	22	23	24
28	29	30	

JULY 2006

SUNDAY	MONDAY	TUESDAY
Notes for July:		
2 O. 2 Sam. 1:1, 17-27 P. Ps. 130 E. 2 Cor. 8:7-15 G. Mark 5:21-43 Green	**3**	**4** Independence Day
9 O. 2 Sam. 5:1-5, 9-10 P. Ps. 48 E. 2 Cor. 12:2-10 G. Mark 6:1-13 Green	**10**	**11**
16 O. 2 Sam. 6:1-5, 12*b*-19 P. Ps. 24 E. Eph. 1:3-14 G. Mark 6:14-29 Green	**17**	**18**
23 O. 2 Sam. 7:1-14*a* P. Ps. 89:20-37 E. Eph. 2:11-22 G. Mark 6:30-34, 53-56 Green	**24**	**25**
30 O. 2 Sam. 11:1-15 P. Ps. 14 E. Eph. 3:14-21 G. John 6:1-21 Green	**31**	

JULY 2006

WEDNESDAY	THURSDAY	FRIDAY	SATURDAY
Notes:			1
5	6	7	8
12	13	14	15
19	20	21	22
26	27	28	29

Notes:

AUGUST 2006

SUNDAY	MONDAY	TUESDAY
Notes for August:		1
6 O. 2 Sam. 11:26–12:13*a* P. Ps. 51:1-12 E. Eph. 4:1-16 G. John 6:24-35 Green	7	8
13 O. 2 Sam. 18:5-9, 15, 31-33 P. Ps. 130 E. Eph. 4:25–5:2 G. John 6:35, 41-51 Green	14	15
20 O. 1 Kings 2:10-12; 3:3-14 P. Ps. 111 E. Eph. 5:15-20 G. John 6:51-58 Green	21	22
27 O. 1 Kings 8:(1, 6, 10-11), 22-30, 41-43 P. Ps. 84 E. Eph. 6:10-20 G. John 6:56-69 Green	28	29

AUGUST 2006

WEDNESDAY	THURSDAY	FRIDAY	SATURDAY
2	3	4	5
9	10	11	12
16	17	18	19
23	24	25	26
30	31	Notes:	

Music Library Card

Library No. ________________ Season(s) ____________________

Title ____

Composer/Arranger ____

Publisher and Publisher's No. ______________________________

Scripture Reference/Theme __________________________________

Instrumentation ____

Voicing ________ Solos _____________ No. of Copies _____

Category ____

Dates Used ____

Other ____

2006

JANUARY 2006

S	M	T	W	T	F	S
1	2	3	4	5	6	7
8	9	10	11	12	13	14
15	16	17	18	19	20	21
22	23	24	25	26	27	28
29	30	31				

FEBRUARY 2006

S	M	T	W	T	F	S
			1	2	3	4
5	6	7	8	9	10	11
12	13	14	15	16	17	18
19	20	21	22	23	24	25
26	27	28				

MARCH 2006

S	M	T	W	T	F	S
			1	2	3	4
5	6	7	8	9	10	11
12	13	14	15	16	17	18
19	20	21	22	23	24	25
26	27	28	29	30	31	

APRIL 2006

S	M	T	W	T	F	S
						1
2	3	4	5	6	7	8
9	10	11	12	13	14	15
16	17	18	19	20	21	22
23	24	25	26	27	28	29
30						

MAY 2006

S	M	T	W	T	F	S
	1	2	3	4	5	6
7	8	9	10	11	12	13
14	15	16	17	18	19	20
21	22	23	24	25	26	27
28	29	30	31			

JUNE 2006

S	M	T	W	T	F	S
				1	2	3
4	5	6	7	8	9	10
11	12	13	14	15	16	17
18	19	20	21	22	23	24
25	26	27	28	29	30	

JULY 2006

S	M	T	W	T	F	S
						1
2	3	4	5	6	7	8
9	10	11	12	13	14	15
16	17	18	19	20	21	22
23	24	25	26	27	28	29
30	31					

AUGUST 2006

S	M	T	W	T	F	S
		1	2	3	4	5
6	7	8	9	10	11	12
13	14	15	16	17	18	19
20	21	22	23	24	25	26
27	28	29	30	31		

SEPTEMBER 2006

S	M	T	W	T	F	S
					1	2
3	4	5	6	7	8	9
10	11	12	13	14	15	16
17	18	19	20	21	22	23
24	25	26	27	28	29	30

OCTOBER 2006

S	M	T	W	T	F	S
1	2	3	4	5	6	7
8	9	10	11	12	13	14
15	16	17	18	19	20	21
22	23	24	25	26	27	28
29	30	31				

NOVEMBER 2006

S	M	T	W	T	F	S
			1	2	3	4
5	6	7	8	9	10	11
12	13	14	15	16	17	18
19	20	21	22	23	24	25
26	27	28	29	30		

DECEMBER 2006

S	M	T	W	T	F	S
					1	2
3	4	5	6	7	8	9
10	11	12	13	14	15	16
17	18	19	20	21	22	23
24	25	26	27	28	29	30
31						

2007

JANUARY 2007

S	M	T	W	T	F	S
	1	2	3	4	5	6
7	8	9	10	11	12	13
14	15	16	17	18	19	20
21	22	23	24	25	26	27
28	29	30	31			

FEBRUARY 2007

S	M	T	W	T	F	S
				1	2	3
4	5	6	7	8	9	10
11	12	13	14	15	16	17
18	19	20	21	22	23	24
25	26	27	28			

MARCH 2007

S	M	T	W	T	F	S
				1	2	3
4	5	6	7	8	9	10
11	12	13	14	15	16	17
18	19	20	21	22	23	24
25	26	27	28	29	30	31

APRIL 2007

S	M	T	W	T	F	S
1	2	3	4	5	6	7
8	9	10	11	12	13	14
15	16	17	18	19	20	21
22	23	24	25	26	27	28
29	30					

MAY 2007

S	M	T	W	T	F	S
		1	2	3	4	5
6	7	8	9	10	11	12
13	14	15	16	17	18	19
20	21	22	23	24	25	26
27	28	29	30	31		

JUNE 2007

S	M	T	W	T	F	S
					1	2
3	4	5	6	7	8	9
10	11	12	13	14	15	16
17	18	19	20	21	22	23
24	25	26	27	28	29	30

JULY 2007

S	M	T	W	T	F	S
1	2	3	4	5	6	7
8	9	10	11	12	13	14
15	16	17	18	19	20	21
22	23	24	25	26	27	28
29	30	31				

AUGUST 2007

S	M	T	W	T	F	S
			1	2	3	4
5	6	7	8	9	10	11
12	13	14	15	16	17	18
19	20	21	22	23	24	25
26	27	28	29	30	31	

SEPTEMBER 2007

S	M	T	W	T	F	S
						1
2	3	4	5	6	7	8
9	10	11	12	13	14	15
16	17	18	19	20	21	22
23	24	25	26	27	28	29
30						

OCTOBER 2007

S	M	T	W	T	F	S
	1	2	3	4	5	6
7	8	9	10	11	12	13
14	15	16	17	18	19	20
21	22	23	24	25	26	27
28	29	30	31			

NOVEMBER 2007

S	M	T	W	T	F	S
				1	2	3
4	5	6	7	8	9	10
11	12	13	14	15	16	17
18	19	20	21	22	23	24
25	26	27	28	29	30	

DECEMBER 2007

S	M	T	W	T	F	S
						1
2	3	4	5	6	7	8
9	10	11	12	13	14	15
16	17	18	19	20	21	22
23	24	25	26	27	28	29
30	31					

2008

JANUARY 2008

S	M	T	W	T	F	S
		1	2	3	4	5
6	7	8	9	10	11	12
13	14	15	16	17	18	19
20	21	22	23	24	25	26
27	28	29	30	31		

FEBRUARY 2008

S	M	T	W	T	F	S
					1	2
3	4	5	6	7	8	9
10	11	12	13	14	15	16
17	18	19	20	21	22	23
24	25	26	27	28	29	

MARCH 2008

S	M	T	W	T	F	S
						1
2	3	4	5	6	7	8
9	10	11	12	13	14	15
16	17	18	19	20	21	22
23	24	25	26	27	28	29
30	31					

APRIL 2008

S	M	T	W	T	F	S
		1	2	3	4	5
6	7	8	9	10	11	12
13	14	15	16	17	18	19
20	21	22	23	24	25	26
27	28	29	30			

MAY 2008

S	M	T	W	T	F	S
				1	2	3
4	5	6	7	8	9	10
11	12	13	14	15	16	17
18	19	20	21	22	23	24
25	26	27	28	29	30	31

JUNE 2008

S	M	T	W	T	F	S
1	2	3	4	5	6	7
8	9	10	11	12	13	14
15	16	17	18	19	20	21
22	23	24	25	26	27	28
29	30					

JULY 2008

S	M	T	W	T	F	S
		1	2	3	4	5
6	7	8	9	10	11	12
13	14	15	16	17	18	19
20	21	22	23	24	25	26
27	28	29	30	31		

AUGUST 2008

S	M	T	W	T	F	S
					1	2
3	4	5	6	7	8	9
10	11	12	13	14	15	16
17	18	19	20	21	22	23
24	25	26	27	28	29	30
31						

SEPTEMBER 2008

S	M	T	W	T	F	S
	1	2	3	4	5	6
7	8	9	10	11	12	13
14	15	16	17	18	19	20
21	22	23	24	25	26	27
28	29	30				

OCTOBER 2008

S	M	T	W	T	F	S
			1	2	3	4
5	6	7	8	9	10	11
12	13	14	15	16	17	18
19	20	21	22	23	24	25
26	27	28	29	30	31	

NOVEMBER 2008

S	M	T	W	T	F	S
						1
2	3	4	5	6	7	8
9	10	11	12	13	14	15
16	17	18	19	20	21	22
23	24	25	26	27	28	29
30						

DECEMBER 2008

S	M	T	W	T	F	S
	1	2	3	4	5	6
7	8	9	10	11	12	13
14	15	16	17	18	19	20
21	22	23	24	25	26	27
28	29	30	31			

Hymn Usage Chart

August 2005 through August 2006

No.	Title	Aug.				Sept.				Oct.					Nov.				Dec.				Jan.					Feb.				Mar.				Apr.					May				June				July					Aug.			
		7	14	21	28	4	11	18	25	2	9	16	23	30	6	13	20	27	4	11	18	25	1	8	15	22	29	5	12	19	26	5	12	19	26	2	9	16	23	30	7	14	21	28	4	11	18	25	2	9	16	23	30	6	13	20	27
	A Charge to Keep I Have																																																								
	A Hymn of Glory Let Us Sing																																																								
	A Mighty Fortress Is Our God																																																								
	A Mother Lined a Basket																																																								
	A Stable Lamp Is Lighted																																																								
	Abide with Me																																																								
	Advent Song																																																								
	Ah, Holy Jesus																																																								
	Alas! and Did My Savior Bleed																																																								
	All Beautiful the March of Days																																																								
	All Creatures of Our God and King																																																								
	All Glory Be to God on High																																																								
	All Glory, Laud, and Honor																																																								
	All Hail King Jesus																																																								
	All Hail the Power of Jesus' Name																																																								
	All I Need Is You																																																								
	All My Heart Today Rejoices																																																								
	All My Hope Is Firmly Grounded																																																								
	All People That on Earth Do Dwell																																																								
	All Praise to Our Redeeming Lord																																																								
	All Praise to Thee, for Thou, O King Divine																																																								
	All Praise to Thee, My God, This Night																																																								
	All the Way My Savior Leads Me																																																								
	All Things Bright and Beautiful																																																								

No.	Title	Aug.				Sept.				Oct.					Nov.				Dec.				Jan.					Feb.				Mar.				Apr.					May				June				July					Aug.			
		7	14	21	28	4	11	18	25	2	9	16	23	30	6	13	20	27	4	11	18	25	1	8	15	22	29	5	12	19	26	5	12	19	26	2	9	16	23	30	7	14	21	28	4	11	18	25	2	9	16	23	30	6	13	20	27
	All Who Hunger																																																								
	All Who Love and Serve Your City																																																								
	All Who Would Valiant Be																																																								
	Alleluia																																																								
	Alleluia (Celtic)																																																								
	Alleluia (Honduras)																																																								
	Alleluia (Taizé)																																																								
	Alleluia! Sing to Jesus!																																																								
	Alleluia, Alleluia																																																								
	Almighty God, Your Word Is Cast																																																								
	Am I a Soldier of the Cross																																																								
	Amazing Grace																																																								
	Amen, Amen																																																								
	Amen, We Praise Your Name, O God																																																								
	America (My Country, 'Tis of Thee)																																																								
	America the Beautiful																																																								
	Amid the Winter's Snow																																																								
	An Outcast Among Outcasts																																																								
	An Upper Room Did Our Lord Prepare																																																								
	And Are We Yet Alive																																																								
	And Can It Be that I Should Gain																																																								
	Angels from the Realms of Glory																																																								
	Angels We Have Heard on High																																																								
	Are Ye Able																																																								
	Arise, Shine																																																								
	Arise, Your Light Is Come																																																								

No.	Title	Aug.				Sept.				Oct.					Nov.				Dec.				Jan.					Feb.				Mar.				Apr.					May				June				July					Aug.			
		7	14	21	28	4	11	18	25	2	9	16	23	30	6	13	20	27	4	11	18	25	1	8	15	22	29	5	12	19	26	5	12	19	26	2	9	16	23	30	7	14	21	28	4	11	18	25	2	9	16	23	30	6	13	20	27
	As a Chalice Cast of Gold																																																								
	As a Fire Is Meant for Burning																																																								
	As Man and Woman We Were Made																																																								
	As the Deer																																																								
	As the Sun Doth Daily Rise																																																								
	As Those of Old Their First Fruits Brought																																																								
	As We Gather																																																								
	As with Gladness Men/Those of Old																																																								
	Ask Ye What Great Thing I Know																																																								
	At the Cross																																																								
	At the Font We Start Our Journey																																																								
	At the Lamb's High Feast We Sing																																																								
	At the Name of Jesus																																																								
	Awake, My Soul, and with the Sun																																																								
	Awake, O Sleeper																																																								
	Away in a Manger																																																								
	Awesome God																																																								
	Baptized in Water																																																								
	Be Known to Us in Breaking Bread																																																								
	Be Still and Know That I Am God																																																								
	Be Still, My Soul																																																								
	Be Thou My Vision																																																								
	Beams of Heaven as I Go																																																								
	Because He Lives																																																								
	Because Thou Hast Said																																																								
	Become to Us the Living Bread																																																								

No.	Title	Aug.				Sept.				Oct.					Nov.				Dec.				Jan.					Feb.				Mar.				Apr.					May				June				July					Aug.			
		7	14	21	28	4	11	18	25	2	9	16	23	30	6	13	20	27	4	11	18	25	1	8	15	22	29	5	12	19	26	5	12	19	26	2	9	16	23	30	7	14	21	28	4	11	18	25	2	9	16	23	30	6	13	20	27
	Behold a Broken World																																																								
	Behold, What Manner of Love																																																								
	Beneath the Cross of Jesus																																																								
	Bind Us Together																																																								
	Bless His Holy Name																																																								
	Bless the Lord																																																								
	Blessed Assurance																																																								
	Blessed Be the God of Israel																																																								
	Blessed Be the Name																																																								
	Blessed Jesus, at Thy Word																																																								
	Blessed Quietness																																																								
	Blest Are They																																																								
	Blest Be the Dear Uniting Love																																																								
	Blest Be the Tie that Binds																																																								
	Blow Ye the Trumpet, Blow																																																								
	Born in the Night																																																								
	Bread of the World																																																								
	Break Forth, O Beauteous Heavenly Light																																																								
	Break Thou the Bread of Life																																																								
	Breathe on Me, Breath of God																																																								
	Brethren, We Have Met to Worship																																																								
	Brightest and Best of the Stars/Sons of the Morning																																																								
	Bring Forth the Kingdom																																																								
	Bring Many Names																																																								
	Broken for Me																																																								
	Built on a Rock																																																								

No.	Title	Aug.				Sept.				Oct.					Nov.				Dec.				Jan.					Feb.				Mar.				Apr.					May				June				July					Aug.			
		7	14	21	28	4	11	18	25	2	9	16	23	30	6	13	20	27	4	11	18	25	1	8	15	22	29	5	12	19	26	5	12	19	26	2	9	16	23	30	7	14	21	28	4	11	18	25	2	9	16	23	30	6	13	20	27
	By Gracious Powers																																																								
	By the Babylonian Rivers																																																								
	Called as Partners in Christ's Service																																																								
	Camina, Pueblo de Dios																																																								
	Cantad al Señor																																																								
	Cantemos al Señor																																																								
	Cares Chorus																																																								
	Carol of the Epiphany																																																								
	Celebrate Love																																																								
	Change My Heart, O God																																																								
	Child of Blessing, Child of Promise																																																								
	Children of the Heavenly Father																																																								
	Christ Beside Me																																																								
	Christ for the World We Sing																																																								
	Christ Has Risen																																																								
	Christ Is Alive																																																								
	Christ Is Made the Sure Foundation																																																								
	Christ Is Risen																																																								
	Christ Is the King!																																																								
	Christ Is the World's Light																																																								
	Christ Jesus Lay in Death's Strong Bands																																																								
	Christ Loves the Church																																																								
	Christ, Mighty Savior																																																								
	Christ the Lord Is Risen																																																								
	Christ the Lord Is Risen Today																																																								
	Christ the Victorious																																																								

No.	Title	Aug.				Sept.				Oct.					Nov.				Dec.				Jan.					Feb.				Mar.				Apr.					May				June				July					Aug.			
		7	14	21	28	4	11	18	25	2	9	16	23	30	6	13	20	27	4	11	18	25	1	8	15	22	29	5	12	19	26	5	12	19	26	2	9	16	23	30	7	14	21	28	4	11	18	25	2	9	16	23	30	6	13	20	27
	Christ, upon the Mountain Peak																																																								
	Christ, When for Us You Were Baptized																																																								
	Christ Whose Glory Fills the Skies																																																								
	Clap your Hands																																																								
	Close to Thee																																																								
	Come and Fill Our Hearts																																																								
	Come and Find the Quiet Center																																																								
	Come and See																																																								
	Come Away with Me																																																								
	Come, All You People																																																								
	Come, and Let Us Sweetly Join																																																								
	Come, Be Baptized																																																								
	Come, Christians, Join to Sing																																																								
	Come! Come! Everybody Worship																																																								
	Come Down, O Love Divine																																																								
	Come, Holy Ghost, Our Souls Inspire																																																								
	Come, Holy Spirit																																																								
	Come, Holy Spirit, Heavenly Dove																																																								
	Come, Labor On																																																								
	Come, Let Us Eat																																																								
	Come, Let Us Join Our Friends Above																																																								
	Come, Let Us Use the Grace Divine																																																								
	Come, Let Us with Our Lord Arise																																																								
	Come, My Way, My Truth, My Life																																																								
	Come Now, O Prince of Peace																																																								
	Come, O Holy Spirit, Come																																																								

No.	Title	Aug.				Sept.				Oct.					Nov.				Dec.				Jan.					Feb.				Mar.				Apr.					May				June				July					Aug.			
		7	14	21	28	4	11	18	25	2	9	16	23	30	6	13	20	27	4	11	18	25	1	8	15	22	29	5	12	19	26	5	12	19	26	2	9	16	23	30	7	14	21	28	4	11	18	25	2	9	16	23	30	6	13	20	27
	Come, O Spirit, Dwell Among Us																																																								
	Come, O Thou Traveler Unknown																																																								
	Come Out the Wilderness																																																								
	Come, Rejoice in God																																																								
	Come, Risen Lord																																																								
	Come, Share the Lord																																																								
	Come, Sinners to the Gospel Feast																																																								
	Come Sunday																																																								
	Come, Thou Almighty King																																																								
	Come, Thou Fount of Every Blessing																																																								
	Come, Thou Long-Expected Jesus																																																								
	Come to the Table																																																								
	Come, We that Love the Lord																																																								
	Come, Ye Disconsolate																																																								
	Come, Ye Faithful, Raise the Strain																																																								
	Come, Ye Sinners, Poor and Needy																																																								
	Come, Ye Thankful People, Come																																																								
	Comfort, Comfort You My People																																																								
	Communion Setting																																																								
	Creating God, Your Fingers Trace																																																								
	Creator God, Creating Still																																																								
	Creator of the Stars of Night																																																								
	Creator Spirit, Come, We Pray																																																								
	Crown Him with Many Crowns																																																								
	Cry of My Heart																																																								
	Cuando El Pobre																																																								

No.	Title	Aug.				Sept.				Oct.					Nov.				Dec.				Jan.					Feb.				Mar.				Apr.					May				June				July					Aug.			
		7	14	21	28	4	11	18	25	2	9	16	23	30	6	13	20	27	4	11	18	25	1	8	15	22	29	5	12	19	26	5	12	19	26	2	9	16	23	30	7	14	21	28	4	11	18	25	2	9	16	23	30	6	13	20	27
	Day Is Done
	Day Is Dying in the West
	De Tierra Lejana Venimos
	Dear Jesus, In Whose Life I See
	Dear Lord and Father of Mankind
	Dear Lord for All in Pain
	Dear Lord, Lead Me Day by Day
	Deck Thyself, My Soul, with Gladness
	Deep in the Shadows of the Past
	Depth of Mercy
	Do, Lord, Remember Me
	Dona Nobis Pacem
	Down at the Cross
	Down to Earth, as a Dove
	Draw Us in the Spirit's Tether
	Earth and All Stars
	Easter People, Raise Your Voices
	Eat This Bread
	El Shaddai
	Emmanuel, Emmanuel
	En El Frió Invernal
	Eternal Father, Strong to Save
	Eternal Light, Shine in My Heart
	Eternal Ruler of the Ceaseless Round
	Eternal Spirit of the Living Christ
	Every Time I Feel the Spirit

No.	Title	Aug.				Sept.				Oct.					Nov.				Dec.				Jan.					Feb.				Mar.				Apr.					May				June				July					Aug.			
		7	14	21	28	4	11	18	25	2	9	16	23	30	6	13	20	27	4	11	18	25	1	8	15	22	29	5	12	19	26	5	12	19	26	2	9	16	23	30	7	14	21	28	4	11	18	25	2	9	16	23	30	6	13	20	27
	Fairest Lord Jesus																																																								
	Faith Is Patience in the Night																																																								
	Faith of Our Fathers																																																								
	Faith, While Trees Are Still in Blossom																																																								
	Father, I Adore You																																																								
	Father, We Praise Thee																																																								
	Father, We Thank You																																																								
	Fight the Good Fight																																																								
	Fill My Cup, Lord																																																								
	Filled with the Spirit's Power																																																								
	Fire of God, Undying Flame																																																								
	Fix Me, Jesus																																																								
	For All the Saints																																																								
	For One Great Peace																																																								
	For the Beauty of the Earth																																																								
	For the Bread Which You Have Broken																																																								
	For the Fruits of This Creation																																																								
	For the Healing of the Nations																																																								
	Forgive Our Sins as We Forgive																																																								
	Forgive Us, Lord																																																								
	Forth in Thy Name, O Lord																																																								
	Forty Days and Forty Nights																																																								
	Forward Through the Ages																																																								
	Freedom Is Coming																																																								
	Freely, Freely																																																								
	From All That Dwell Below the Skies																																																								
	From Heaven Above																																																								
	From the Rising of the Sun																																																								

No.	Title	Aug.				Sept.				Oct.					Nov.				Dec.				Jan.					Feb.				Mar.				Apr.					May				June				July					Aug.			
		7	14	21	28	4	11	18	25	2	9	16	23	30	6	13	20	27	4	11	18	25	1	8	15	22	29	5	12	19	26	5	12	19	26	2	9	16	23	30	7	14	21	28	4	11	18	25	2	9	16	23	30	6	13	20	27
	Gather Us In																																																								
	Gentle Mary Laid Her Child																																																								
	Give Me a Clean Heart																																																								
	Give Me the Faith Which Can Remove																																																							
	Give Peace																																																								
	Give Thanks for Life																																																								
	Give Thanks with a Grateful Heart																																																								
	Give to the Winds Thy Fears																																																							
	Give to Us Your Peace																																																								
	Gloria, Gloria																																																								
	Glorify Thy Name																																																								
	Glorious Things of Thee Are Spoken																																																								
	Glory Be to Jesus																																																								
	Glory Be to the Father																																																								
	Glory to God																																																								
	Glory to God in the Highest																																																								
	Go Down, Moses																																																								
	Go Forth for God																																																								
	Go, Make of All Disciples																																																								
	Go Now in Peace																																																								
	Go, Tell It on the Mountain																																																								
	Go to Dark Gethsemane																																																								
	Go Ye, Go Ye into the World																																																								
	God Be in My Head																																																								
	God Be with You till We Meet Again																																																								
	God Claims You																																																								
	God Created Heaven and Earth																																																								

No.	Title	Aug.				Sept.				Oct.					Nov.				Dec.				Jan.					Feb.				Mar.				Apr.					May				June				July					Aug.			
		7	14	21	28	4	11	18	25	2	9	16	23	30	6	13	20	27	4	11	18	25	1	8	15	22	29	5	12	19	26	5	12	19	26	2	9	16	23	30	7	14	21	28	4	11	18	25	2	9	16	23	30	6	13	20	27
	God Hath Spoken by the Prophets																																																								
	God, How Can We Forgive																																																								
	God Is Here Today																																																								
	God Is So Good																																																								
	God Made from One Blood																																																								
	God Moves in a Mysterious Way																																																								
	God of Grace and God of Glory																																																								
	God of Many Names																																																								
	God of Our Life																																																								
	God of the Ages/Our Fathers																																																								
	God of the Prophets																																																								
	God of the Sparrow God of the Whale																																																								
	God, That Madest Earth and Heaven																																																								
	God the Omnipotent																																																								
	God the Sculptor of the Mountains																																																								
	God the Spirit, Guide and Guardian																																																								
	God Weeps																																																								
	God, Who Stretched the Spangled Heavens																																																								
	God, Who Touches Earth with Beauty																																																								
	God, Whose Almighty Word																																																								
	God, Whose Giving Knows No Ending																																																								
	God, Whose Love Is Reigning O'er Us																																																								
	God, Whose Purpose Is to Kindle																																																								
	God Will Take Care of You																																																								
	God, You Are My God																																																								
	Good Christian Friends/Men Rejoice																																																								

No.	Title	Aug.				Sept.				Oct.					Nov.				Dec.				Jan.					Feb.				Mar.				Apr.					May				June				July					Aug.			
		7	14	21	28	4	11	18	25	2	9	16	23	30	6	13	20	27	4	11	18	25	1	8	15	22	29	5	12	19	26	5	12	19	26	2	9	16	23	30	7	14	21	28	4	11	18	25	2	9	16	23	30	6	13	20	27
	Good Christians All, Rejoice and Sing!																																																								
	Goodness Is Stronger than Evil																																																								
	Grace Alone																																																								
	Grace Greater Than Our Sin																																																								
	Gracious Spirit, Holy Ghost																																																								
	Great God, We Sing That Mighty Hand																																																								
	Great Is the Lord																																																								
	Great Is Thy Faithfulness																																																								
	Greet Now the Swiftly Changing Year																																																								
	Guide Me, O My/Thou Great Redeemer/Jehovah																																																								
	Guide My Feet																																																								
	Hail the Day That Sees Him Rise																																																								
	Hail Thee, Festival Day																																																								
	Hail, Thou Once Despised Jesus																																																								
	Hail to the Lord's Anointed																																																								
	Halle, Halle, Halleluja																																																								
	Hallelujah! What a Savior																																																								
	Happy the Home When God Is There																																																								
	Hark! the Herald Angels Sing																																																								
	Hark, the Glad Sound																																																								
	Have Thine Own Way, Lord																																																								
	He Came Down																																																								
	He Has Made Me Glad																																																								
	He Is Born																																																								
	He Is Exalted																																																								

No.	Title	Aug.				Sept.				Oct.					Nov.				Dec.				Jan.					Feb.				Mar.				Apr.					May				June				July					Aug.			
		7	14	21	28	4	11	18	25	2	9	16	23	30	6	13	20	27	4	11	18	25	1	8	15	22	29	5	12	19	26	5	12	19	26	2	9	16	23	30	7	14	21	28	4	11	18	25	2	9	16	23	30	6	13	20	27
	He Is Lord																																																								
	He Leadeth Me: O Blessed Thought																																																								
	He Lives																																																								
	He Never Said a Mumbalin' Word																																																								
	He Rose																																																								
	He Touched Me																																																								
	He Who Began a Good Work in You																																																								
	Heal Me, Hands of Jesus																																																								
	Heal Us, Emmanuel, Hear Our Prayer																																																								
	Healer of Our Every Ill																																																								
	Heleluyan																																																								
	Help Us Accept Each Other																																																								
	Herald, Sound the Note of Judgment																																																								
	Heralds of Christ																																																								
	Here Am I																																																								
	Here I Am, Lord																																																								
	Here Is Bread, Here Is Wine																																																								
	Here, O Lord, Your Servants Gather																																																								
	Here, O My Lord, I See Thee																																																								
	His Eye Is on the Sparrow																																																								
	His Name Is Wonderful																																																								
	Hitsuji wa nemureri																																																								
	Holy																																																								
	Holy Ghost, Dispel Our Sadness																																																								
	Holy God, We Praise Thy Name																																																								
	Holy Ground																																																								
	Holy, Holy																																																								

No.	Title	Aug.				Sept.				Oct.					Nov.				Dec.				Jan.					Feb.				Mar.				Apr.					May				June				July					Aug.			
		7	14	21	28	4	11	18	25	2	9	16	23	30	6	13	20	27	4	11	18	25	1	8	15	22	29	5	12	19	26	5	12	19	26	2	9	16	23	30	7	14	21	28	4	11	18	25	2	9	16	23	30	6	13	20	27
	Holy, Holy, Holy																																																						
	Holy, Holy, Holy Lord																																																						
	Holy Spirit, Come, Confirm Us																																																						
	Holy Spirit, Come to Us																																																						
	Holy Spirit, Truth Divine																																																						
	Honor and Praise																																																						
	Hope of the World																																																						
	Hosanna																																																						
	Hosanna! Hosanna!																																																						
	How Blest Are They Who Trust in Christ																																																						
	How Can We Name a Love																																																						
	How Can We Sinners Know																																																						
	How Firm a Foundation																																																						
	How Good, Lord, to Be Here																																																						
	How Great Our Joy																																																						
	How Great Thou Art																																																						
	How Like a Gentle Spirit																																																						
	How Long, O Lord																																																						
	How Lovely, Lord, How Lovely																																																						
	How Majestic Is Thy/Your Name																																																						
	How Shall They Hear the Word of God																																																						
	How Sweet the Name of Jesus Sounds																																																						
	Humble Thyself/Yourself in the Sight of the Lord																																																						
	Hymn of Promise																																																						
	I Am the Light of the World																																																						
	I Am Thine, O Lord																																																						
	I Am Your Mother																																																						

No.	Title	Aug.				Sept.				Oct.					Nov.				Dec.				Jan.					Feb.				Mar.				Apr.					May				June				July					Aug.			
		7	14	21	28	4	11	18	25	2	9	16	23	30	6	13	20	27	4	11	18	25	1	8	15	22	29	5	12	19	26	5	12	19	26	2	9	16	23	30	7	14	21	28	4	11	18	25	2	9	16	23	30	6	13	20	27
	I Bind unto Myself Today																																																								
	I Cast All My Cares																																																								
	I Come with Joy																																																								
	I Have Decided to Follow Jesus																																																								
	I Heard the Voice of Jesus Say																																																								
	I Know that My Redeemer Lives																																																								
	I Know Whom I Have Believed																																																								
	I Love the Lord, Who Heard My Cry																																																								
	I Love Thy Kingdom, Lord																																																								
	I Love to Tell the Story																																																								
	I Love You, Lord																																																								
	I Must Tell Jesus																																																								
	I Need Thee Every Hour																																																								
	I Sing a Song of the Saints of God																																																								
	I Sing Praises to Your Name																																																								
	I Sing the Almighty Power of God																																																								
	I Sought the Lord																																																								
	I Stand Amazed in the Presence																																																								
	I Surrender All																																																								
	I Want a Principle Within																																																								
	I Want Jesus to Walk with Me																																																								
	I Want to Be Ready																																																								
	I Want to Walk as a Child of the Light																																																								
	I Was There to Hear Your Borning Cry																																																								
	I Will Call upon the Lord																																																								
	I Will Trust in the Lord																																																								
	If It Had Not Been For the Lord																																																								

No.	Title	Aug.				Sept.				Oct.					Nov.				Dec.				Jan.					Feb.				Mar.				Apr.					May				June				July					Aug.			
		7	14	21	28	4	11	18	25	2	9	16	23	30	6	13	20	27	4	11	18	25	1	8	15	22	29	5	12	19	26	5	12	19	26	2	9	16	23	30	7	14	21	28	4	11	18	25	2	9	16	23	30	6	13	20	27
	If Thou But Suffer God to Guide Thee																																																								
	I'll Fly Away																																																								
	I'll Praise My Maker																																																								
	I'm Goin'a Sing When the Spirit Says Sing																																																								
	I'm Gonna Live So God Can Use Me																																																								
	I'm So Glad Jesus Lifted Me																																																								
	Immortal, Invisible, God Only Wise																																																								
	In Bethlehem a Newborn Boy																																																								
	In Christ There Is No East or West																																																								
	In His Time																																																								
	In Remembrance of Me																																																								
	In the Bleak Midwinter																																																								
	In the Cross of Christ I Glory																																																								
	In the Garden																																																								
	In the Lord I'll Be Ever Thankful																																																								
	In the Midst of New Dimensions																																																								
	In the Singing																																																								
	In Thee Is Gladness																																																								
	In Unity We Lift Our Song																																																								
	Infant Holy, Infant Lowly																																																								
	Into My Heart																																																								
	Isaiah the Prophet Has Written of Old																																																								
	It Came upon the Midnight Clear																																																								
	It Is Well with My Soul																																																								
	It's Me, It's Me, O Lord																																																								
	I've Got Peace Like a River																																																								
	I've Just Come from the Fountain																																																								

No.	Title	Aug.				Sept.				Oct.					Nov.				Dec.				Jan.					Feb.				Mar.				Apr.					May				June				July					Aug.			
		7	14	21	28	4	11	18	25	2	9	16	23	30	6	13	20	27	4	11	18	25	1	8	15	22	29	5	12	19	26	5	12	19	26	2	9	16	23	30	7	14	21	28	4	11	18	25	2	9	16	23	30	6	13	20	27
	Jerusalem the Golden																																																								
	Jesus Be Praised																																																								
	Jesus, Draw Me Close																																																								
	Jesus, Keep Me Near the Cross																																																								
	Jesus, Lord, We Look to Thee																																																								
	Jesus, Lover of My Soul																																																								
	Jesus Loves Me																																																								
	Jesus, Name Above All Names																																																								
	Jesus, Priceless Treasure																																																								
	Jesus, Remember Me																																																								
	Jesus, Savior, Pilot Me																																																								
	Jesus Shall Reign																																																								
	Jesus, Stand Among Us																																																								
	Jesus, Tempted in the Desert																																																								
	Jesus! the Name High Over All																																																								
	Jesus, the Very Thought of Thee																																																								
	Jesus, Thine All-Victorious Love																																																								
	Jesus, Thou Joy of Loving Hearts																																																								
	Jesus, United by Thy Grace																																																								
	Jesus Walked This Lonesome Valley																																																								
	Jesus, We Are Here																																																								
	Jesus, We Want to Meet																																																								
	Jesus! What a Friend for Sinners																																																								
	Jesus' Hands Were Kind Hands																																																								
	Joseph Dearest, Joseph Mine																																																								
	Joy Comes with the Dawn																																																								

No.	Title	Aug.				Sept.				Oct.					Nov.				Dec.				Jan.					Feb.				Mar.				Apr.					May				June				July					Aug.			
		7	14	21	28	4	11	18	25	2	9	16	23	30	6	13	20	27	4	11	18	25	1	8	15	22	29	5	12	19	26	5	12	19	26	2	9	16	23	30	7	14	21	28	4	11	18	25	2	9	16	23	30	6	13	20	27
	Joy in the Morning																																																								
	Joy to the World																																																								
	Joyful, Joyful, We Adore Thee																																																								
	Just a Closer Walk with Thee																																																								
	Just as I Am, Without One Plea																																																								
	King of Kings																																																								
	Kum Ba Yah																																																								
	Kyrie																																																								
	Kyrie Eleison																																																								
	Lamb of God																																																								
	Lead Me, Guide Me																																																								
	Lead Me, Lord																																																								
	Lead Me to Calvary																																																								
	Lead On, O Cloud of Presence																																																								
	Lead On, O King Eternal																																																								
	Leaning on the Everlasting Arms																																																								
	Leave It There																																																								
	Let All Mortal Flesh Keep Silence																																																								
	Let All the World in Every Corner Sing																																																								
	Let All Things Now Living																																																								
	Let It Breathe on Me																																																								
	Let Jesus Come into Your Heart																																																								
	Let My People Seek Their Freedom																																																								
	Let the Whole Creation Cry																																																								
	Let There Be Light																																																								

No.	Title	Aug.				Sept.				Oct.					Nov.				Dec.				Jan.					Feb.				Mar.				Apr.					May				June				July					Aug.			
		7	14	21	28	4	11	18	25	2	9	16	23	30	6	13	20	27	4	11	18	25	1	8	15	22	29	5	12	19	26	5	12	19	26	2	9	16	23	30	7	14	21	28	4	11	18	25	2	9	16	23	30	6	13	20	27
	Let There Be Peace on Earth																																																						
	Let Us Be Bread																																																							
	Let Us Break Bread Together																																																							
	Let Us Now Depart in Thy Peace																																																							
	Let Us Offer to the Father																																																							
	Let Us Plead for Faith Alone																																																							
	Let Us Talents and Tongues Employ																																																							
	Let Us with a Gladsome/Joyful Mind																																																							
	Let Us with a Joyful Mind																																																							
	Life-Giving Bread																																																							
	Lift Every Voice and Sing																																																							
	Lift High the Cross																																																							
	Lift Up Your Heads, Ye Mighty Gates																																																							
	Light of the World																																																							
	Like a Child																																																							
	Like the Murmur of the Dove's Song																																																							
	Live in Charity																																																							
	Living for Jesus																																																							
	Lo, He Comes with Clouds Descending																																																							
	Lo, How a Rose E'er Blooming																																																							
	Lonely the Boat																																																							
	Look, Ye Saints! The Sight Is Glorious																																																							
	Lord, Be Glorified																																																							
	Lord Christ, When First You Came to Earth																																																							
	Lord, Dismiss Us with Thy Blessing																																																							
	Lord, Enthroned in Heavenly Splendor																																																							

No.	Title	Aug.				Sept.				Oct.					Nov.				Dec.				Jan.					Feb.				Mar.				Apr.					May				June				July					Aug.			
		7	14	21	28	4	11	18	25	2	9	16	23	30	6	13	20	27	4	11	18	25	1	8	15	22	29	5	12	19	26	5	12	19	26	2	9	16	23	30	7	14	21	28	4	11	18	25	2	9	16	23	30	6	13	20	27
	Lord God, Almighty																																																								
	Lord God, Your Love Has Called Us Here																																																								
	Lord, Have Mercy																																																								
	Lord, I Lift Your Name on High																																																								
	Lord, I Want to Be a Christian																																																								
	Lord Jesus, Think on Me																																																								
	Lord, Listen to Your Children																																																								
	Lord, Listen to Your Children Praying																																																								
	Lord, Make Us Servants of Your Peace																																																								
	Lord of All Good																																																								
	Lord of All Hopefulness																																																								
	Lord of the Dance																																																								
	Lord of the Living																																																								
	Lord, Speak to Me																																																								
	Lord, We Come to Ask Your Blessing																																																								
	Lord, Who Throughout These Forty Days																																																								
	Lord, Whose Love Through Humble Service																																																								
	Lord, You Give the Great Commission																																																								
	Love Came Down at Christmas																																																								
	Love Divine, All Loves Excelling																																																								
	Love the Lord Your God																																																								
	Loving Spirit																																																								
	Majesty, Worship His Majesty																																																								
	Make Me a Captive, Lord																																																								
	Make Me a Channel of Your Peace																																																								

No.	Title	Aug.				Sept.				Oct.					Nov.				Dec.				Jan.					Feb.				Mar.				Apr.					May				June				July					Aug.			
		7	14	21	28	4	11	18	25	2	9	16	23	30	6	13	20	27	4	11	18	25	1	8	15	22	29	5	12	19	26	5	12	19	26	2	9	16	23	30	7	14	21	28	4	11	18	25	2	9	16	23	30	6	13	20	27
	Make Me a Servant																																																								
	Make Us One																																																								
	Maker in Whom We Live																																																								
	Mantos y Palmas																																																								
	Many and Great, O God																																																								
	Many Are the Lightbeams																																																								
	Many Gifts, One Spirit																																																								
	Marching to Zion																																																								
	Masithi																																																								
	May the Grace of Christ Our Savior																																																								
	May You Run and Not Be Weary																																																								
	More Like You																																																								
	More Love to Thee, O Christ																																																								
	More Precious than Silver																																																								
	Morning Glory, Starlit Sky																																																								
	Morning Has Broken																																																								
	Mothering God, You Gave Me Birth																																																								
	Mountains Are All Aglow																																																								
	Must Jesus Bear the Cross Alone																																																								
	My Faith Looks Up to Thee																																																								
	My God, How Wonderful You Are																																																								
	My God, I Love Thee																																																								
	My Gratitude Now Accept, O God																																																								
	My Hope Is Built																																																								
	My Jesus, I Love Thee																																																								
	My Life Flows on in Endless Song																																																								

No.	Title	Aug.				Sept.				Oct.					Nov.				Dec.				Jan.					Feb.				Mar.				Apr.					May				June				July					Aug.			
		7	14	21	28	4	11	18	25	2	9	16	23	30	6	13	20	27	4	11	18	25	1	8	15	22	29	5	12	19	26	5	12	19	26	2	9	16	23	30	7	14	21	28	4	11	18	25	2	9	16	23	30	6	13	20	27
	My Life Is in You, Lord																																																								
	My Lord, What a Morning/Mourning																																																								
	My Master See, the Time Has Come																																																								
	My Prayer Rises to Heaven																																																								
	My Shepherd Will Supply My Need																																																								
	My Song Is Love Unknown																																																								
	My Soul Gives Glory to My God																																																								
	My Tribute																																																								
	Near to the Heart of God																																																								
	Nearer, My God, to Thee																																																								
	Niño Lindo																																																								
	New Songs of Celebration Render																																																								
	Nobody Know the Trouble I See																																																								
	Not for Tongues of Heaven's Angels																																																								
	Not So in Haste, My Heart																																																								
	Nothing Betweem																																																								
	Nothing but the Blood																																																								
	Nothing Can Trouble																																																								
	Now It Is Evening																																																								
	Now Let Us from This Table Rise																																																								
	Now Praise the Hidden God of Love																																																								
	Now Thank We All Our God																																																								
	Now the Day Is Over																																																								
	Now the Green Blade Riseth																																																								
	Now the Silence																																																								
	Now, on Land and Sea Descending																																																								

No.	Title	Aug.				Sept.				Oct.					Nov.				Dec.				Jan.					Feb.				Mar.				Apr.					May				June				July					Aug.			
		7	14	21	28	4	11	18	25	2	9	16	23	30	6	13	20	27	4	11	18	25	1	8	15	22	29	5	12	19	26	5	12	19	26	2	9	16	23	30	7	14	21	28	4	11	18	25	2	9	16	23	30	6	13	20	27
	O Blessed Spring																																																								
	O Breath of Life																																																								
	O Christ, the Healer																																																								
	O Church of God, United																																																								
	O Come, All Ye Faithful																																																								
	O Come and Dwell in Me																																																								
	O Come, O Come, Emmanuel																																																								
	O Day of God, Draw Nigh																																																								
	O Day of Peace That Dimly Shines																																																								
	O Day of Radiant Gladness																																																								
	O Food to Pilgrims Given																																																								
	O For a Closer Walk with God																																																								
	O For a Heart to Praise My God																																																								
	O For a Thousand Tongues to Sing																																																								
	O For a World																																																								
	O Freedom																																																								
	O Gladsome Light																																																								
	O God Beyond All Praising																																																								
	O God in Heaven																																																								
	O God of Bethel by Whose Hand																																																								
	O God of Earth and Altar																																																								
	O God of Every Nation																																																								
	O God of Love, O God of Peace																																																								
	O God, Our Help in Ages Past																																																								
	O God, We Bear the Imprint of Your Face																																																								
	O God, What You Ordain Is Right																																																								

No.	Title	Aug.				Sept.				Oct.					Nov.				Dec.				Jan.					Feb.				Mar.				Apr.					May				June				July					Aug.			
		7	14	21	28	4	11	18	25	2	9	16	23	30	6	13	20	27	4	11	18	25	1	8	15	22	29	5	12	19	26	5	12	19	26	2	9	16	23	30	7	14	21	28	4	11	18	25	2	9	16	23	30	6	13	20	27
	O God Who Shaped Creation																																																				
	O God, You Give Humanity Its Name																																																				
	O Happy Day, That Fixed My Choice																																																				
	O Holy City, Seen of John																																																				
	O Holy Radiance, Joyous Light																																																				
	O Holy Spirit, by Whose Breath																																																				
	O Holy Spirit, Root of Life																																																				
	O How He Loves You and Me																																																				
	O How I Love Jesus																																																				
	O Jesus Christ, May Grateful Hymns Be Rising																																																				
	O Jesus, I Have Promised																																																				
	O Jesus, My King																																																				
	O Little Town of Bethlehem																																																				
	O Look and Wonder																																																				
	O Lord, Hear My Prayer																																																				
	O Lord, How Shall I Meet You																																																				
	O Lord, May Church and Home Combine																																																				
	O Lord, You're Beautiful																																																				
	O Lord, Your Tenderness																																																				
	O Love Divine, What Hast Thou Done																																																				
	O Love, How Deep																																																				
	O Love That Wilt Not Let Me Go																																																				
	O Mary, Don't You Weep																																																				
	O Master, Let Me Walk with Thee																																																				
	O Morning Star, How Fair and Bright																																																				
	O My Soul, Bless God the Father/Your Redeemer																																																				
	O Perfect Love																																																					

No.	Title	Aug.				Sept.				Oct.					Nov.				Dec.				Jan.					Feb.				Mar.				Apr.					May				June				July					Aug.			
		7	14	21	28	4	11	18	25	2	9	16	23	30	6	13	20	27	4	11	18	25	1	8	15	22	29	5	12	19	26	5	12	19	26	2	9	16	23	30	7	14	21	28	4	11	18	25	2	9	16	23	30	6	13	20	27
	O Praise the Gracious Power																																																								
	O Radiant Light, O Sun Divine																																																								
	O Sacred Head, Now Wounded																																																								
	O Sing a Song of Bethlehem																																																								
	O Sons and Daughters, Let Us Sing																																																								
	O Spirit of the Living God																																																								
	O Splendor of God's Glory Bright																																																								
	O That I Had a Thousand Voices																																																								
	O the Depth of Love Divine																																																								
	O the Lamb																																																								
	O Thou, in Whose Presence																																																								
	O Thou Who Camest from Above																																																								
	O Thou Who This Mysterious Bread																																																								
	O What Their Joy and Their Glory Must Be																																																								
	O Wondrous Sight! O Vision Fair																																																								
	O Word of God Incarnate																																																								
	O Worship the King																																																								
	O Young and Fearless Prophet																																																								
	O Zion, Haste																																																								
	Of All the Spirit's Gifts to Me																																																								
	Of the Father's Love Begotten																																																								
	Oh, I Know the Lord's Laid His Hands on Me																																																								
	On Eagle's Wings																																																								
	On Jordan's Bank the Baptist's Cry																																																								
	On Pentecost They Gathered																																																								
	On the Day of Resurrection																																																								
	On This Day Earth Shall Ring																																																								

No.	Title	Aug.				Sept.				Oct.					Nov.				Dec.				Jan.					Feb.				Mar.				Apr.					May				June				July					Aug.			
		7	14	21	28	4	11	18	25	2	9	16	23	30	6	13	20	27	4	11	18	25	1	8	15	22	29	5	12	19	26	5	12	19	26	2	9	16	23	30	7	14	21	28	4	11	18	25	2	9	16	23	30	6	13	20	27
	Once in Royal David's City																																																								
	One Bread, One Body																																																								
	One God and Father of Us All																																																								
	One Holy Night in Bethlehem																																																								
	Only Trust Him																																																								
	Only-Begotten, Word of God Eternal																																																								
	Onward, Christian Soldiers																																																								
	Open My Eyes, That I May See																																																								
	Open Now Thy Gates of Beauty																																																								
	Open Our Eyes, Lord																																																								
	Our God Reigns																																																								
	Our God, to Whom We Turn																																																								
	Our Parent, by Whose Name																																																								
	Out of the Depths I Cry to Thee/You																																																								
	Over My Head																																																								
	Pass It On																																																								
	Pass Me Not, O Gentle Savior																																																								
	People, Look East																																																								
	People Need the Lord																																																								
	Please Enter My Heart, Hosanna																																																								
	Praise and Thanksgiving Be to God																																																								
	Praise God, from Whom All Blessings Flow																																																								
	Praise, My Soul, the King of Heaven																																																								
	Praise Our God Above																																																								
	Praise, Praise, Praise the Lord																																																								
	Praise the Lord, God's Glories Show																																																								

No.	Title	Aug.				Sept.				Oct.					Nov.				Dec.				Jan.					Feb.				Mar.				Apr.					May				June				July					Aug.			
		7	14	21	28	4	11	18	25	2	9	16	23	30	6	13	20	27	4	11	18	25	1	8	15	22	29	5	12	19	26	5	12	19	26	2	9	16	23	30	7	14	21	28	4	11	18	25	2	9	16	23	30	6	13	20	27
	Praise the Lord Who Reigns Above																																																								
	Praise the Lord with the Sound of Trumpet																																																								
	Praise the Lord! Ye Heavens, Adore Him																																																								
	Praise the Name of Jesus																																																								
	Praise the Source of Faith and Learning																																																								
	Praise the Spirit in Creation																																																								
	Praise to the Lord																																																								
	Praise to the Lord, the Almighty																																																								
	Praise Ye the Lord																																																								
	Praise You																																																								
	Prayer Is the Soul's Sincere Desire																																																								
	Prayers of the People																																																								
	Precious Lord, Take My Hand																																																								
	Precious Name																																																								
	Prepare the Way of the Lord																																																								
	Pues Si Vivimos																																																								
	Refiner's Fire																																																								
	Rejoice in God's Saints																																																								
	Rejoice! Rejoice, Believers																																																								
	Rejoice, the Lord Is King																																																								
	Rejoice, Ye Pure in Heart																																																								
	Rescue the Perishing																																																								
	Ride On! Ride On in Majesty																																																								
	Rise, Shine, You People																																																								
	Rise to Greet the Sun																																																								

No.	Title	Aug.				Sept.				Oct.					Nov.				Dec.				Jan.					Feb.				Mar.				Apr.					May				June				July					Aug.			
		7	14	21	28	4	11	18	25	2	9	16	23	30	6	13	20	27	4	11	18	25	1	8	15	22	29	5	12	19	26	5	12	19	26	2	9	16	23	30	7	14	21	28	4	11	18	25	2	9	16	23	30	6	13	20	27
	Rise Up, O Men of God																																																								
	Rise Up, Shepherd, and Follow																																																								
	Rock of Ages, Cleft for Me																																																								
	Rock-a-Bye, My Dear Little Boy																																																								
	Sacred the Body																																																								
	Said Judas to Mary																																																								
	Sanctuary																																																								
	Saranam, Saranam																																																								
	Savior, Again to Thy Dear Name																																																								
	Savior, Like a Shepherd Lead Us																																																								
	Savior of the Nations, Come																																																								
	Savior, Who Dying Gave																																																								
	See How Great a Flame Aspires																																																								
	See the Morning Sun Ascending																																																								
	See the Lord																																																								
	Seek Ye First																																																								
	Send Me, Lord																																																								
	Send Your Word																																																								
	Sent Forth by God's Blessing																																																								
	Sent Out in Jesus' Name																																																								
	Serenity																																																								
	Shall We Gather at the River																																																								
	Shalom Chaverim																																																								
	Shalom to You																																																								
	She Comes Sailing on the Wind																																																								

No.	Title	Aug.				Sept.				Oct.					Nov.				Dec.				Jan.					Feb.				Mar.				Apr.					May				June				July					Aug.			
		7	14	21	28	4	11	18	25	2	9	16	23	30	6	13	20	27	4	11	18	25	1	8	15	22	29	5	12	19	26	5	12	19	26	2	9	16	23	30	7	14	21	28	4	11	18	25	2	9	16	23	30	6	13	20	27
	Shepherd Me, O God																																																							
	Shine, Jesus, Shine																																																							
	Shout to the Lord																																																							
	Silence, Frenzied, Unclean Spirit																																																							
	Silent Night, Holy Night																																																							
	Since Jesus Came into My Heart																																																							
	Sing a New Song to the Lord																																																							
	Sing Alleluia to the Lord																																																							
	Sing, My Tongue, the Glorious Battle																																																							
	Sing of Mary, Pure and Lowly																																																							
	Sing Praise to God Who Reigns Above																																																							
	Sing Praise to the Lord																																																							
	Sing to the Lord of the Harvest																																																							
	Sing We Now of Christmas																																																							
	Sing with All the Saints in Glory																																																							
	Softly and Tenderly Jesus Is Calling																																																							
	Sois la Semilla																																																							
	Soldiers of Christ, Arise																																																							
	Something Beautiful																																																							
	Song of Hope																																																							
	Songs of Praise the Angels Sang																																																							
	Songs of Thankfulness and Praise																																																							
	Soon and Very Soon																																																							
	Source and Sovereign, Rock and Cloud																																																							
	Spirit Divine, Attend Our Prayers																																																							
	Spirit of Faith, Come Down																																																							

No.	Title	Aug.				Sept.				Oct.					Nov.				Dec.				Jan.					Feb.				Mar.				Apr.					May				June				July					Aug.			
		7	14	21	28	4	11	18	25	2	9	16	23	30	6	13	20	27	4	11	18	25	1	8	15	22	29	5	12	19	26	5	12	19	26	2	9	16	23	30	7	14	21	28	4	11	18	25	2	9	16	23	30	6	13	20	27
	Spirit of God																																																								
	Spirit of God, Descend upon My Heart																																																								
	Spirit of God, Unleashed on Earth																																																								
	Spirit of the Living God																																																								
	Spirit Song																																																								
	Spirit, Spirit of Gentleness																																																								
	Stand by Me																																																								
	Stand Up and Bless the Lord																																																								
	Stand Up, Stand Up for Jesus																																																								
	Standing on the Promises																																																								
	Star-Child																																																								
	Stay with Me																																																								
	Stay with Us																																																								
	Steal Away to Jesus																																																								
	Such Perfect Love My Shepherd Shows																																																								
	Sunday's Palms Are Wednesday's Ashes																																																								
	Surely the Presence of the Lord																																																								
	Sweet Delight, Most Lovely																																																								
	Sweet Hour of Prayer																																																								
	Sweet, Sweet Spirit																																																								
	Swiftly Pass the Clouds of Glory																																																								
	Swing Low, Sweet Chariot																																																								
	Take My Life, and Let It Be Consecrated																																																								
	Take Our Bread																																																								
	Take Time to Be Holy																																																								

No.	Title	Aug.				Sept.				Oct.					Nov.				Dec.				Jan.					Feb.				Mar.				Apr.					May				June				July					Aug.			
		7	14	21	28	4	11	18	25	2	9	16	23	30	6	13	20	27	4	11	18	25	1	8	15	22	29	5	12	19	26	5	12	19	26	2	9	16	23	30	7	14	21	28	4	11	18	25	2	9	16	23	30	6	13	20	27
	Take Up Thy Cross																																																								
	Taste and See																																																								
	Teach Me, My God and King																																																								
	Tell Me the Stories of Jesus																																																								
	Tell Out, My Soul																																																								
	Thank You, God, for Water, Soil, and Air																																																								
	Thank You, Jesus																																																								
	Thank You, Lord																																																								
	Thanks to God Whose Word Was Written																																																								
	That Boy-Child of Mary																																																								
	That Easter Day with Joy Was Bright																																																								
	The Angel Gabriel from Heaven Came																																																								
	The Battle Hymn of the Republic																																																								
	The Blood Will Never Lose Its Power																																																								
	The Bread of Life for All Is Broken																																																								
	The Care the Eagle Gives Her Young																																																								
	The Church of Christ, in Every Age																																																								
	The Church's One Foundation																																																								
	The Day of Resurrection																																																								
	The Day Thou Gavest, Lord, Is Ended																																																								
	The Family Prayer Song																																																								
	The Friendly Beasts																																																								
	The First Noel																																																								
	The First One Ever																																																								
	The First Song of Isaiah																																																								

No.	Title	Aug.				Sept.				Oct.					Nov.				Dec.				Jan.					Feb.				Mar.				Apr.					May				June				July					Aug.			
		7	14	21	28	4	11	18	25	2	9	16	23	30	6	13	20	27	4	11	18	25	1	8	15	22	29	5	12	19	26	5	12	19	26	2	9	16	23	30	7	14	21	28	4	11	18	25	2	9	16	23	30	6	13	20	27
	The Fragrance of Christ																																																								
	The Gift of Love																																																								
	The Glory of These Forty Days																																																								
	The God of Abraham Praise																																																								
	The Head That Once Was Crowned																																																								
	The King of Glory Comes																																																								
	The King of Love My Shepherd Is																																																								
	The King Shall Come When Morning Dawns																																																								
	The Lily of the Valley																																																								
	The Lone, Wild Bird																																																								
	The Lord Bless and Keep You																																																								
	The Lord's My Shepherd, I'll Not Want																																																								
	The Lord's Prayer																																																								
	The Old Rugged Cross																																																								
	The People Who in Darkness Walked																																																								
	The Royal Banners Forward Fly/Go																																																								
	The Servant Song																																																								
	The Snow Lay on the Ground																																																								
	The Spirit Sends Us Forth to Serve																																																								
	The Star-Spangled Banner																																																								
	The Steadfast Love of the Lord																																																								
	The Strife Is O'er, the Battle Done																																																								
	The Summons																																																								
	The Trees of the Field																																																								
	The Virgin Mary Had a Baby Boy																																																								

No.	Title	Aug.				Sept.				Oct.					Nov.				Dec.				Jan.					Feb.				Mar.				Apr.					May				June				July					Aug.			
		7	14	21	28	4	11	18	25	2	9	16	23	30	6	13	20	27	4	11	18	25	1	8	15	22	29	5	12	19	26	5	12	19	26	2	9	16	23	30	7	14	21	28	4	11	18	25	2	9	16	23	30	6	13	20	27
	The Voice of God Is Calling																																																								
	There Are Some Things I May Not Know																																																								
	There Is a Balm in Gilead																																																								
	There Is a Fountain Filled with Blood																																																								
	There Is a Green Hill Far Away																																																								
	There's a Song																																																								
	There's a Spirit in the Air																																																								
	There's a Voice in the Wilderness																																																								
	There's a Wideness in God's Mercy																																																								
	There's Something About That Name																																																								
	There's Within My Heart a Melody																																																								
	They'll Know We Are Christians by Our Love																																																								
	Thine Be the Glory																																																								
	This Is a Day of New Beginnings																																																								
	This Is My Father's World																																																								
	This Is My Song																																																								
	This Is the Day																																																								
	This Is the Feast of Victory																																																								
	This Is the Spirit's Entry Now																																																								
	This Joyful Eastertide																																																								
	This Little Light of Mine																																																								
	Thou Art Worthy																																																								
	Thou Didst Leave Thy Throne																																																								
	Thou Hidden Love of God																																																								
	Thou Hidden Source of Calm Repose																																																								
	Through It All																																																								

No.	Title	Aug.				Sept.				Oct.					Nov.				Dec.				Jan.					Feb.				Mar.				Apr.					May				June				July					Aug.			
		7	14	21	28	4	11	18	25	2	9	16	23	30	6	13	20	27	4	11	18	25	1	8	15	22	29	5	12	19	26	5	12	19	26	2	9	16	23	30	7	14	21	28	4	11	18	25	2	9	16	23	30	6	13	20	27
	Thy Holy Wings, O Savior																																																								
	Thy Strong Word																																																								
	Thy Word Is a Lamp																																																								
	Time Now to Gather																																																								
	'Tis Finished! the Messiah Dies																																																								
	'Tis So Sweet to Trust in Jesus																																																								
	'Tis the Gift																																																								
	'Tis the Old Ship of Zion																																																								
	To a Maid Engaged to Joseph																																																								
	To God Be the Glory																																																								
	To Know You More																																																								
	To Mock Your Reign, O Dearest Lord																																																								
	Toda la Tierra																																																								
	Together We Serve																																																								
	Touch the Earth Lightly																																																								
	Trust and Obey																																																								
	Tú Has Venido a la Orilla																																																								
	Turn Your Eyes upon Jesus																																																								
	'Twas in the Moon of Wintertime																																																								
	Two Fishermen																																																								
	Ubi Caritas																																																								
	Una Espiga																																																								
	Unsettled World																																																								
	Unto Us a Boy Is Born																																																								
	Up from the Grave He Arose																																																								

No.	Title	Aug.				Sept.				Oct.					Nov.				Dec.				Jan.					Feb.				Mar.				Apr.					May				June				July					Aug.			
		7	14	21	28	4	11	18	25	2	9	16	23	30	6	13	20	27	4	11	18	25	1	8	15	22	29	5	12	19	26	5	12	19	26	2	9	16	23	30	7	14	21	28	4	11	18	25	2	9	16	23	30	6	13	20	27
	Victim Divine																																																								
	Victory in Jesus																																																								
	Wade in the Water																																																								
	Wake, Awake, for Night Is Flying																																																								
	Walk with Me																																																								
	Wash, O God, Our Sons and Daughters																																																								
	Watchman, Tell Us of the Night																																																								
	Water, River, Spirit, Grace																																																								
	We All Are One in Mission																																																								
	We Are Called																																																								
	We Are Climbing Jacob's Ladder																																																								
	We Are God's People																																																								
	We Are Marching/Singing																																																								
	We Are One in Christ Jesus																																																								
	We Are the Body of Christ																																																								
	We Are the Church																																																								
	We Believe in One True God																																																								
	We Bring the Sacrifice of Praise																																																								
	We Gather Together																																																								
	We Give Thee But Thine Own																																																								
	We Have Come at Christ's Own Bidding																																																								
	We Know That Christ Is Raised																																																								
	We Live/Walk by Faith and Not By Sight																																																								
	We Meet You, O Christ																																																								
	We Need a Faith																																																								

No.	Title	Aug.				Sept.				Oct.					Nov.				Dec.				Jan.					Feb.				Mar.				Apr.					May				June				July					Aug.			
		7	14	21	28	4	11	18	25	2	9	16	23	30	6	13	20	27	4	11	18	25	1	8	15	22	29	5	12	19	26	5	12	19	26	2	9	16	23	30	7	14	21	28	4	11	18	25	2	9	16	23	30	6	13	20	27
	We Plow the Fields and Scatter																																																								
	We Praise You, O God, Our Redeemer																																																								
	We Sang Our Glad Hosannas																																																								
	We Shall Overcome																																																								
	We Sing of Your Glory																																																								
	We Sing to You, O God																																																								
	We Three Kings																																																								
	We Thy People, Praise Thee																																																								
	We Utter Our Cry																																																								
	We Walk by Faith																																																								
	We Were Baptized in Christ Jesus																																																								
	We Who Would Valiant Be																																																								
	We Will Glorify the King of Kings																																																								
	We Worship and Adore You																																																								
	We Would See Jesus																																																								
	We'll Understand It Better By and By																																																								
	Weary of All Trumpeting																																																								
	Welcome, Happy Morning																																																								
	Wellspring of Wisdom																																																								
	Were You There																																																								
	We've a Story to Tell to the Nations																																																								
	What a Friend We Have in Jesus																																																								
	What a Mighty God We Serve																																																								
	What Child Is This																																																								
	What Does the Lord Require of You																																																								
	What Gift Can We Bring																																																								

No.	Title	Aug.				Sept.				Oct.					Nov.				Dec.				Jan.					Feb.				Mar.				Apr.					May				June				July					Aug.			
		7	14	21	28	4	11	18	25	2	9	16	23	30	6	13	20	27	4	11	18	25	1	8	15	22	29	5	12	19	26	5	12	19	26	2	9	16	23	30	7	14	21	28	4	11	18	25	2	9	16	23	30	6	13	20	27
	What Star Is This, with Beams So Bright																																																								
	What Wondrous Love Is This																																																								
	When All Your Mercies, O My God																																																								
	When Cain Killed Abel																																																								
	When Christmas Morn Is Dawning																																																								
	When God Restored Our Common Life																																																								
	When I Survey the Wondrous Cross																																																								
	When in Our Music God Is Glorified																																																								
	When Jesus Came to Jordan																																																								
	When Jesus the Healer Passed Through Galilee																																																								
	When Jesus Wept																																																								
	When Love Is Found																																																								
	When Morning Gilds the Skies																																																								
	When Our Confidence Is Shaken																																																								
	When the Church of Jesus																																																								
	When We All Get to Heaven																																																								
	When We Are Called to Sing Your Praise																																																								
	When Will People Cease Their Fighting?																																																								
	Where Charity and Love Prevail																																																								
	Where Children Belong																																																								
	Where Cross the Crowded Ways of Life																																																								
	Where He Leads Me																																																								
	Where the Spirit of the Lord Is																																																								
	While Shepherds Watched Their Flocks																																																								
	Who Is He in Yonder Stall																																																								
	Who Is My Mother, Who Is My Brother																																																								
	Whom Shall I Send?																																																								

No.	Title	Aug.				Sept.				Oct.					Nov.				Dec.				Jan.					Feb.				Mar.				Apr.					May				June				July					Aug.			
		7	14	21	28	4	11	18	25	2	9	16	23	30	6	13	20	27	4	11	18	25	1	8	15	22	29	5	12	19	26	5	12	19	26	2	9	16	23	30	7	14	21	28	4	11	18	25	2	9	16	23	30	6	13	20	27
	Why Has God Forsaken Me?																																																								
	Why Stand So Far Away, My God?																																																								
	Why We Sing																																																								
	Wild and Lone the Prophet's Voice																																																								
	Wind Who Makes All Winds That Blow																																																								
	Within the Day-to-Day																																																								
	Without Seeing You																																																								
	Woke Up This Morning																																																								
	Women in the Night																																																								
	Womb of Life																																																								
	Wonder of Wonders, Here Revealed																																																								
	Wonderful Words of Life																																																								
	Word of God, Come Down on Earth																																																								
	Would I Have Answered When You Called																																																								
	Wounded World that Cries for Healing																																																								
	Ye Servants of God																																																								
	Ye Watchers and Ye Holy Ones																																																								
	Ye Who Claim the Faith of Jesus																																																								
	You Alone Are Holy																																																								
	You Are Mine																																																								
	You Are My Hiding Place																																																								
	You Are the Way																																																								
	You Are Worthy																																																								
	You Have Put On Christ																																																								
	You Satisfy the Hungry Heart																																																								
	You Who Are Thirsty																																																								

No.	Title	Aug.				Sept.				Oct.					Nov.				Dec.				Jan.					Feb.				Mar.				Apr.					May				June				July					Aug.			
		7	14	21	28	4	11	18	25	2	9	16	23	30	6	13	20	27	4	11	18	25	1	8	15	22	29	5	12	19	26	5	12	19	26	2	9	16	23	30	7	14	21	28	4	11	18	25	2	9	16	23	30	6	13	20	27
	Your Love, O God, Has Called Us Here																																																								
	Your Loving Kindness Is Better Than Life																																																								

ADDITIONAL SELECTIONS

Children's Choir Registration Form

Child's Name: ______________________________

Parents' Name: ______________________________

Address: ______________________________

City, State, ZIP+4: ______________________________

Home Phone No.: ______________ Work Phone No.: ______________

Home FAX No.: ______________ Work FAX No.: ______________

Cell Phone No.: ______________ Other No.: ______________

E-Mail: ______________________________

Birthday: ______________________________

School attending: ______________________Year in school: __________

Check the musical group(s) in which you participate:

___ Older Children ___ Younger Children ___ Pre-school ___ Choir Parent

___ Children's Handbell Choir ___ __________ ___ __________

Complete only applicable information below:

Instrument(s) played: ______________________________

How many years? ______________________________

Taking lessons now? __________ If so, teacher's name: ______________

Choir parents only:

___ Available during rehearsals ___ Help with parties ___ Can send snacks

___ Help with transportation ___ Help with costumes ___ Trip chaperone

___ Help with anything!

In case of emergency, notify:

Name: ______________________ Phone No.: ______________

Relationship to child: ______________________________

CHILDREN

Rehearsal Planning Worksheet for a Children's Choir

CHILDREN

Choir Name ______________________________

Rehearsal Date and Time ______________________________

Musical concepts in this rehearsal:

Spiritual/worship concepts in this rehearsal:

Activities to enhance learning of concepts:

Preparation/supplies needed:

1. Prerehearsal/arrival activities:

2. Opening prayer:

3. Vocal warm-ups:

4. Anthem(s)/hymn(s)/song(s) in preparation for next worship service and related teaching plans:

5. Music to continue learning (for future services) and related teaching plans:

6. New material to be introduced and related teaching plans:

7. Announcements:

8. Devotional and closing prayer (led by ______________________________):

9. Take home (reminders, handouts):

10. Comments:

Event (anthem, announcement, devotional)	Time to begin	Comment

Recruitment Letter to a Child

Dear LaKrishia:

"Then Sings My Soul"—what does that mean? That means that there is something special that happens when we join together to sing our praises to God. It's something that happens that makes you just glow with joy when you sing! Is that cool or what? I hope you will be a part of the Cherub Choir at St. Mathias Church this year.

We are going to have really great year in choir this year. We need you as a part of the choir to make it even better! What will we do? We will learn songs and stories about Jesus and about how we can follow God in our life. Our first rehearsal is Wednesday, September 6. Choir rehearsal begins at 6:45 P.M. and we have planned special activities for you as soon as you arrive.

Come and be a part of the choir. Let's join our voices together to discover how much God has filled our souls!

With thanks to God for you,
(Choir Director's Name)

Recruitment Letter to Parents of Children

Dear Steve and Camilla:

I am looking forward to the opportunity to working with your child in choir at Cornerstone Church this year. What will we do in rehearsal? During choir rehearsals your child will learn hymns, anthems, and other music for worship. We will hear and sing scripture songs. No prior experience is needed to sing in a choir at Cornerstone Church, just a willingness to learn!

Choir registration will be held on Sunday, September 10. You will find the registration table at the Welcome Center. Additionally, there will be many opportunities for you to help me throughout the choir year. I hope that you will volunteer. See the choir registration form for information.

For many children, singing in choir is the beginning of a life filled with service to God through the use of their gifts and talents. The commitment to attending rehearsals, the chance to learn and improve music skills, to worship God, and the friendships that come as the children sing, play, and have fun together is an important foundation for a lifetime of involvement in the church. The music and the faith formation that happens during a choir year will help your child discover what it means when we say "then sings my soul!"

Singing praises to God,
(Choir Director's Name)

Missed You (Child)

Dear Jonathan:

We missed you at choir rehearsal this week. We just didn't have the same sparkle in our choir without you. I hope that everything is OK with you. We all hope to see you at rehearsal next week Wednesday, September 27, at 6:45 P.M. What did we do in rehearsal last night? We worked really hard on our song *(insert song title here)* and also had fun *(insert other activities you did at rehearsal).*

We worked on our music, remembering that when we raise our voices together we are filling our souls with praise to God. We hope that you will help us next week.

With thanks to God for you,
(Choir Director's Name)

Attendance Reminder: Children's Choir Parents

Dear Jennifer and Steve:

The Trinity Singers will be leading in worship at Gordon Church for the first time for this choir year on Sunday, October 9, at the 8:30 A.M. service. We will be singing *(insert anthem title here).*

We will meet at 8:00 A.M. on Sunday morning in the choir room for a short rehearsal. You will want to sit near the front during worship this Sunday so your child can be assured that you are in worship to hear them sing.

If your child does not have a robe assigned, please call *(insert name)* at *(insert phone)* to arrange to meet before our rehearsal to time to get fitted for a choir robe. Parent Helpers are always needed to assist in helping the choir on the Sundays they sing; helping kids find their places in choir, passing out instruments, and so on. Please call me to volunteer! Let's work together to help your child discover how much God has filled their souls!

Singing praises to God,
(Choir Director's Name)

Happy Birthday (Child)

Dear Lindsey:

It's your special day! Happy Birthday! I'm sure you will have a wonderful day. Having you in my choir is a joy. You are one of the reasons my soul sings praises to God. I give thanks to God for your presence in my life. Celebrate this day!

Singing praises to God for you,
(Choir Director's Name)

Clip Art

Adult/Youth Choir Registration Form

Name: ____________________

Address: ____________________

City, State, ZIP+4: ____________________

Home Phone No.: ____________________ Work Phone No.: ____________________

Home FAX No.: ____________________ Work FAX No.: ____________________

Cell Phone No.: ____________________ Other No.: ____________________

E-mail: ____________________

Birthday: ____________________

ADULT/YOUTH

Check the musical group(s) in which you participate:

___ Chancel Choir	___ Adult Handbells	___ Worship Team	___ Praise Band
___ Youth Choir	___ Youth Handbells	___ Church Band/Orchestra	
___ ___________	___ ___________	___ ___________	___ ___________

Complete only applicable information below:

(Circle one) Soprano 1 Soprano 2 Alto 1 Alto 2 Tenor 1 Tenor 2 Bass 1 Bass 2

Instrument(s) played:

___ Piccolo	___ Alto Sax	___ Baritone Horn	___ Piano/Synth.
___ Flute	___ Tenor Sax	___ Tuba	___ Acoustic Guitar
___ Oboe	___ Baritone Sax	___ Violin	___ Electric Guitar
___ Clarinet	___ French Horn	___ Viola	___ Bass Guitar
___ Bass Clarinet	___ Trumpet	___ 'Cello	___ Percussion/Trap Set
___ Bassoon	___ Bass Trombone	___ String Bass	___ Organ

How many years? ____________________

Taking lessons now? __________ If so, teacher's name: ____________________

School attending: ____________________ Year in school: __________

In case of emergency, notify:

Name: ____________________ Phone No.: ____________________

Relationship: ____________________

Rehearsal Planning Worksheet for an Adult Choir

Choir Name ______________________________

Rehearsal Date and Time ______________________________

1. Prerehearsal/arrival activities:

2. Vocal warm-ups:

3. Music for worship this week (including hymns, choruses, descants, responses, anthems):

4. Music to continue learning (for future services):

5. New music to introduce:

6. Announcements:

7. Devotional and closing prayer (led by ______________________________):

8. Things to do (resources needed for rehearsal, new music to be distributed, music that should be pulled from folders, and so on):

9. Comments:

ADULT/YOUTH

Event (anthem, announcement, devotional)	Time to begin	Comment

Rehearsal Date ______________________ Preparation for ______________________

Rehearsal Planning Worksheet for a Youth Choir

Choir Name ______________________________

Rehearsal Date and Time: ______________________________

1. Prerehearsal/arrival activities:
   Musical concepts in this rehearsal:

   Spiritual/worship concepts in this rehearsal:

   Preparation/supplies needed:

ADULT/YOUTH

2. Opening prayer:

3. Vocal warm-ups:

4. Music in preparation for next worship service:

5. Music to continue learning (in preparation for future worship services):

6. New music to introduce:

7. Announcements:

8. Devotional and closing prayer (led by ______________________________):

9. Things to do (resources needed for rehearsal, new music to be distributed, music that should be pulled from folders, and so on):

10. Comments:

Event (anthem, announcement, devotional)	Time to begin	Comment

ADULT/YOUTH

Adult Recruitment Letter

Dear Nancy:

"Then sings my soul!" There are times when this phrase simply describes it best. Those times we are filled joy, those times we are filled with uncertainty or sorrow. There are times when music and song can help us share what is deep in our soul.

I am asking you to join others at First Church in sharing your gift and talent with us in the *(insert name of choir)*. It doesn't matter if you've sung in a choir for many years or never have sung in a choir before—we want to learn to sing praises and worship God together with you.

Come and let the music fill you until your spirit is revived and renewed. The *(insert name of choir)* rehearses on Wednesday evenings from 6:30–8:00 P.M. in the Music Suite. No prior experience is needed, just a willingness to learn. Please join us this week.

If you have any questions about the music ministry, please call me at 555-1234 or e-mail me at music@firstchurch.org.

Won't you come and join us as we share our music to tell how great God is?

Singing praises to God,
(Choir Director's Name)

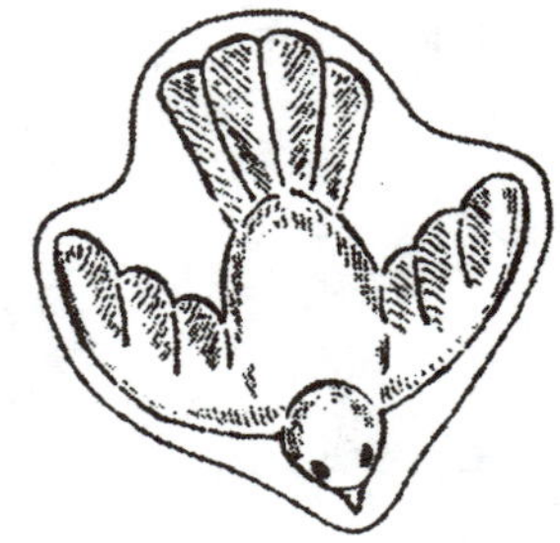

Clip Art

Then
Sings
My
Soul

Happy Birthday (Adult)

Dear EJ:

Your birthday is a day to celebrate! The members of (insert choir name) and I wish you a Happy Birthday. You are one of the reasons my soul sings praises to God. I give thanks to God for your presence in my life.

Sing God's praise this day and let your soul be filled!

Singing praises to God,
(Choir Director's Name)

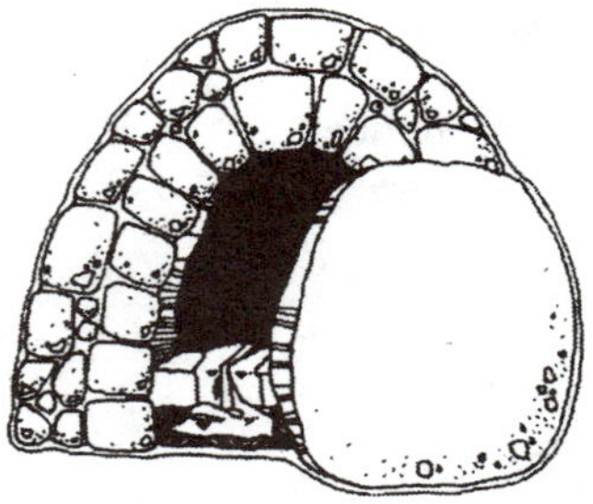

Clip Art

Missed You (Adult)

Dear Adam:

You were missed this week. You were included in our prayers during our rehearsal. I hope to see you this week as we lead in the 11:00 A.M. worship service. Our anthem for this Sunday, December 10 will be *(insert name of anthem)*. Please call me at *(insert phone number)* if you have any questions.

Join us next week so we can sing and renew our spirits together! Sing God's praise this day and let your soul be filled!

Singing praises to God,
(Choir Director's Name)

Clip Art

Clip Art

Then Sings My Soul

Happy Birthday (Youth Choir)

Dear Matthew:

What? It's your birthday? No way! Well, we'll just have to celebrate! I'm just bursting with excitement that today is your special day! I am *thankful* that you are a part of the Youth Choir. I praise God that you have chosen to share you gifts and talents with us. I know —here's a new way of thinking about our S.O.U.L.!

Singing
On this, your special day
Uniquely gifted by God—that's you!
Loved by God and all of us too!

Happy Birthday!

Singing praises to God,
(Choir Director's Name)

Missed You (Youth)

Dear Ariel:

our anthem is really sounding good but it would have been even better if you had been singing it with us. i missed being with you in choir this week and i hope to see you next week. We included you in our prayers during rehearsal. call me at *(insert Phone number)* or e-mail me at music@Aldersgatechurch.org and let me know how you are doing this week.

Join us next week so we can our sing and renew our spirit together! Remember we've got SOUL in our choir!

Singing praises to God,
(choir Director's Name)

Recruitment Letter to a Youth

Dear Kristen:

"Then sings my soul"—what in the world does that mean? There are times when this phrase simply describes it best. Those times when we are filled joy, those times when we are filled with uncertainty or sorrow. There are times when music and songs can help us share what is deep in our soul. Just consider how SOUL fits into our Youth Choir ministry!

Singing
Opening our hearts to feel God's presence
Using our gifts and talents
Laughing, caring, and praying together

I am hoping that you will choose to join the Youth Choir at Calvary Church this year. I believe that you need to share your gift and talents with others at church. I know that God has already given you the tools you need to do that—your voice!

Join others from church as we work together to serve God through music—as we sing in worship and use our voices in sharing God's word. We'll learn and grow together in our faith though our music—we'll feed out souls!

Join me for our first rehearsal on Sunday, September 10, at 4:00 P.M. in the Choir Room. Call or e-mail me if you have any questions at *(insert phone and e-mail address here).*

Singing praises to God,
(Choir Director's Name)

Clip Art

Attendance Reminder for Youth

Dear Sam:

Don't forget! We sing this Sunday, January 14, for the 11:00 A.M. service. Meet with the rest of the Bethlehem Church Youth Choir in the choir room at 10:30 A.M. for our warm-up and to review the music for the service. We will sing (insert name of anthem). Come and share a part of your S.O.U.L. this week in worship!

Singing
Opening our hearts to feel God's presence
Using our gifts and talents
Laughing, caring, and praying together

Singing praises to God,
(Choir Director's Name)

Clip Art

Sing unto the Lord a new song.

Rehearsal Planning Worksheet for Handbell Choir or Instrumental Ensemble

Choir Name ____

Rehearsal Date ______________________ Preparation for ______________________

1. Prerehearsal/arrival activities:

2. Technical exercises, warm-ups (tuning):

3. Music for next worship (including service music, hymns, descants, anthem accompaniment):

4. Music to continue learning (for future services):

5. New music to be introduced:

6. Announcements:

7. Devotional and closing prayer (led by ____):

8. Things to do (resources needed for rehearsal, new music to be distributed, music that should be pulled from folders):

9. Comments:

Event (anthem, announcement, devotional)	Time to begin	Comment

Attendance Reminder (Handbell Choir/Instrumental)

On Sunday, April 15 *(insert name of choir/ensemble)* will be leading in worship. We will meet in the sanctuary at 10:00 A.M. to warm up and to review our music. You will be able to sit with your families after we lead in worship. I need some help in setting up the equipment for worship. Please call or e-mail me *(insert phone number, e-mail)* if you are able to help prior to our warm-up time. Wear your outfits for the services. Thank you for your hard work and I look forward to seeing you there.

Ring your bells! Play your horns and drums! Let your soul be filled!

Sing praises to God,
(Choir Director's Name)

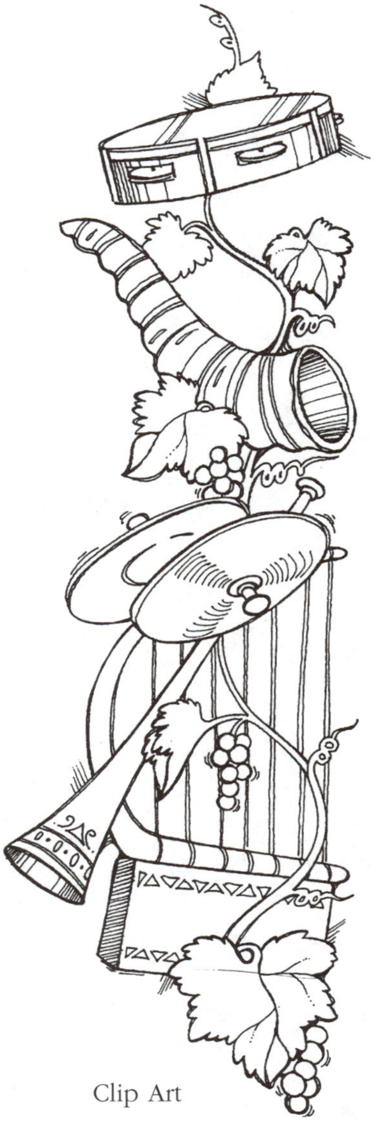

Clip Art

Missed You (Handbell Choir/Instrumental)

Dear Kendall:

We missed you in *(insert name of choir/ensemble)* rehearsal this week. You are such an important part of our group, that we just aren't the same without you. I do hope to see you next week in our rehearsal. We worked hard on our music for the Bell Festival. Call or e-mail me *(insert phone number, e-mail address)* and let me know how you are doing.

Ring your bells! Play your horns and drums! Let your soul be filled!

Singing praises to God,
(Choir Director's Name)

Clip Art

Recruitment Letter to Bell Choir/Instrumental

Dear Jere and Kris:

Welcome to Huntington Street Church. The theme for our Music Ministry this year is "then sings my soul." Those of us who play bells and instruments also say, "then *plays* my soul." While we may have changed the text a little, you know how much music can help fill our souls. There are those times when we are filled joy, those times when we are filled with uncertainty or sorrow. There are times when music and songs can help us share what is deep in our soul.

I'd like to invite you to join us this year in the music ministry by sharing your gift in music. Here are the specifics about *(insert bell choir/instrumental ensemble name):*

Rehearsal Day: Thursdays, beginning September 14
Time: 7:00–8:30 P.M.
Place: Choir Room
Other information: *(Insert specifics to your setting.)*

I will call you soon to answer any questions you may have. Ring your bells! Play your horns and drums! Let your soul be filled! Join us this year!

Singing praises to God,
(Choir Director's Name)

Instrument and Equipment Inventory and Maintenance Chart

Duplicate this form as needed. Place it in a file folder along with the receipt, item warranty and service information, and other information pertinent to this item.

Item ______________________________ Serial/ID No. ______________

Manufacturer ______________________ Where Purchased ______________

Date Purchased __________ Price __________ Location of Item ______________

Contact Name ______________________ Phone Number ______________

Address __________________ City __________ State ____ Zip ________

Maintenance Record

Date	Maintenance

FORMS/CHARTS

Music Department Budget Form

Instrument Maintenance

Sanctuary organ tuning: ______(tunings per year) x ____________ (cost per tuning) = ____________________

Sanctuary piano tuning: ______(tunings per year) x ____________ (cost per tuning) = ____________________

Additional pianos: ______ (number of pianos) x __________ (tunings per year) x (cost per tuning) = ________

List location of each piano in the church:

Additional maintenance costs (piano regulation, organ adjustments, repairs): ____________________________

Handbell maintenance:

Service contract visit cost: ________________

Weekly cleaning supplies:

Polish: ______________________________

Polishing cloths: ______________________

Instruments

New Instruments: ____

New Instruments: ____

Supplies: ____

Total Instrument Maintenance Costs: ____

Music

Group Name	Anticipated Music Needs	Approximate Cost

Subtotal: ____________________

Organ music supplement (money designated to defray expense of purchasing new music for the organist):

____

Total Music Costs:__________________________________

Guest Musicians

Substitute organist/director: ________(estimated number of days needed) x ________(fee/service) = ________

Guest musicians (for major works and/or Christmas/Easter):

Cantata/Anthem/Work to be performed	Musicians needed	Cost

______________ (cost per player) x ________ (number of players) = ______________

Total Guest Musician Costs: ______________

Miscellaneous Expenses

Purchase small instruments, teaching aids, musical supplies (folders, postcards), handbell gloves, and so on. Itemize anticipated purchases and estimate cost involved.

Total Miscellaneous Expenses: ______________

Continuing Education

Registration fees for choir festivals, choir camp, and other events: ______________

List each event and the costs involved:

Registration fees for leadership to attend workshops, training events, and conferences:

____

List each event and the costs involved:

Total Continuing Education Expenses: ______________

Additional Expenses

This category is unique to your music program. Include any additional expenses you may incur during the coming year. Itemize each purchase, including the estimated cost.

Total Additional Expenses: ______________

Total Music Budget (add subtotals): ______________

FORMS/CHARTS

Music Department Budget Summary

	Budget Current Year	Proposed Budget	Increase/(Decrease)
Instrument Maintenance			
Organ tunings			
Piano tunings			
Additional maintenance			
Handbell maintenance			
Music			
Purchase new music			
Organ music supplement			
Guest Musicians			
Substitute organist/director			
Guest musicians			
Miscellaneous Expenses			
(Itemize planned purchases.)			
Continuing Education			
Registration fees			
Leadership training events			
Additional expenses			
(Itemize based on your program.)			
TOTAL			

Explanation of significant increases/decreases:

FORMS/CHARTS

List each musical group in your music department. Estimate the cost of purchasing new music for each group. Be sure to include any major purchase, such as a children's musical.

Choir Robe Assignment Chart

Robe Number	Name

Choir Folder Assignment Chart

Folder Number	Name

Choir Robe and Folder Assignment Chart

Robe Number	Name	Folder Number

Members of________________________________Choir

2005-2006 Attendance Record

Name	Address and zip code	Home Phone	Work Phone	Month and Date of Birth	AUGUST '05	SEPTEMBER '05	OCTOBER '05	NOVEMBER '05

	AUGUST '05	SEPTEMBER '05	OCTOBER '05	NOVEMBER '05
Members Present				
Leader(s) Present				
New Members Present (Not included in above total)				
TOTAL PRESENT				
MEMBERS ABSENT				

Place Dates in Top Triangles
Check (✓) When Present

Example:

1 / 4	8 / 11	15 / 18	22 / 25	29 / 1
✓	✓	✓ ✓	✓ ✓	✓

Children/Youth in______________________________Choir

2005-2006 Attendance Record

Name	Address and zip code	Home Phone	Work Phone	Grade	Month and Date of Birth	AUGUST '05	SEPTEMBER '05	OCTOBER '05	NOVEMBER '05

	AUGUST '05	SEPTEMBER '05	OCTOBER '05	NOVEMBER '05
Members Present				
Leader(s) Present				
New Members Present (Not included in above total)				
TOTAL PRESENT				
MEMBERS ABSENT				

Place Dates in Top Triangles
Check (✓) When Present
Example:

1 / 4	8 / 11	15 / 18	22 / 25	29 / 1
/ ✓	✓ /	✓ / ✓	✓ / ✓	/ ✓

(Second page)

Place Dates in Top Triangles
Check (✓) When Present

2005-2006 Attendance Record

DECEMBER '05	JANUARY '06	FEBRUARY '06	MARCH '06	APRIL '06	MAY '06	JUNE '06	JULY '06	AUGUST '06	NOTES
									Members Present
									Leader(s) Present
									New Members Present (Not included in above total)
									TOTAL PRESENT
									MEMBERS ABSENT

In Recognition of

This certificate is awarded to

____

at _______________________________

Date ______________ ______________

Then Sings My Soul

Evaluation Form

Please complete the following questionnaire about this resource. Suggestions will be used to develop future editions of *The Choir Director's Organizer.*

Name____

Address____

____

E-mail: ____

Church Size: ____ 0-100 members
____ 100-500 members
____ 500-1,000 members
____ Over 1,000 members

Lectionary Use: My church DOES DOES NOT (circle one) use the Revised Common Lectionary on a regular basis.

The Organizer's Format:
I found the printed format of the Organizer to be
___ of little help. ___ of moderate help. ___ of great help.
Suggestions: ____

Worship Music Planners:
I found the worship music planners to be ___ of little help. ___ of moderate help. ___ of great help.
Suggestions: ____

Rehearsal Planning Worksheets:
I found the rehearsal planning worksheets to be
___ of little help. ___ of moderate help. ___ of great help.
Suggestions: ____

Choir Registration Forms
I found the choir registration forms to be ___ of little help. ___ of moderate help. ___ of great help.
Suggestions: ____

Sample Letters:
I found the sample letters to be ___ of little help. ___ of moderate help. ___ of great help.
Suggestions: ____

Clip Art:
I found the clip art to be
___ of little help. ___ of moderate help. ___ of great help.
Suggestions:

Hymn Usage Chart:
I found the hymn usage chart to be ___ of little help. ___ of moderate help. ___ of great help.
Suggestions: ____

Instrument and Equipment Forms:
I found the instrument and equipment forms to be
___ of little help. ___ of moderate help. ___ of great help.

Music Department Budget Forms:
I found the music department budget forms to be
___ of little help. ___ of moderate help. ___ of great help.

Choir Robe and Folder Assignment Charts:
I found the choir robe and folder assignment charts to be
___ of little help. ___ of moderate help. ___ of great help.

Attendance Records:
I found the attendance records to be ___ of little help. ___ of moderate help. ___ of great help.
Suggestions: ____

Choir Theme Suggestions:____________________________

Further Comments and Suggestions: ____________________

Send to: **Music Resources, Attn.: Editor**, The United Methodist Publishing House, 201 Eighth Avenue, South, Nashville, TN 37203.